DAVID L. DAMBRE

Renegade

Defying My Father's Opposition To Work For The Pentagon

Copyright © 2022 by David L. Dambre

All rights reserved. No part of this publication may be reproduced, stored or transmitted in any form or by any means, electronic, mechanical, photocopying, recording, scanning, or otherwise without written permission from the publisher. It is illegal to copy this book, post it to a website, or distribute it by any other means without permission.

David L. Dambre asserts the moral right to be identified as the author of this work.

First edition

ISBN 979-8-218-02280-8

Cover art by Roy Kamau

This book was professionally proofread, formatted, and typeset by Roy Kamau.

Contents

Preface	iv
Acknowledgement	vi
1 Voices from Afar	1
2 My Year as a Slave	24
3 A New Adventure in Kumasi	57
4 Indentured in America	84
5 Attending University	104
About the Author	121

Preface

I began writing this book during the COVID-19 lockdown when I was conducting my work as Africa Desk Director at the Pentagon from home. I was working on my Professional Doctoral degree, but mainly I was thinking back on my life, as my current isolation—just me and my fiancée rambling through a large house in the Maryland suburbs—reminded me of the old isolation growing up in a remote village of the West African country of Togo, a country not even on the radar of many Westerners. And though my current isolation was different, because, in Togo, I was the king's grandson and surrounded by my large family of 200+, there was something about how alone I felt in Togo, how different I felt from my siblings and age mates, and how alone I later felt as a young man living in Ghana, that tugged at me.

The more this thought tugged at me, the more I felt I needed to write a book. The book appeared clearly in my mind starting with my initial desire to go to elementary school, leading through the loss of my father, exploring tough times in my life in Ghana, recalling my immigration to the U.S., and finally, culminating with success: a high paying job in my field at the Pentagon, a nearly completed dissertation, and on the verge of marrying a woman who shared my religious beliefs. On paper, I had it all.

But for others in West Africa, the story had not ended so well. I still had siblings, friends, and people I'd never met, calling me on WhatsApp. Many Africans believed that when they arrived in America, everything would be waiting for them. Traffickers used this strategy to get money from those desperate to emigrate. The traffickers would say, "The government is going to get you a job. The government is going to feed you. They're going to get you a house." The traffickers would make emigrants feel so excited, that they wouldn't think about anything else except handing over the money to the people who could help them get there.

Herta, for instance, came to the U.S. on a student visa. Before she left *Namibia,* people were telling her, "When you go to America, you don't even have to take any clothes. You just get yourself there, and everything will be waiting for you. There are so many clothes, so many things." When she arrived, she found out that wasn't true. In fact, it was nothing like that. She had to fight for herself.

As an immigrant, the very first person you meet in America either helps you grow into a better person or destroys your life. Someone who wants to help you will tell you to do the things they didn't do, and help you avoid their mistakes. But if you meet the other kind of person, one who has gone through something so terrible that they will want you to have to experience it too, then watch out. Instead of trying to prevent you from going through it, they intentionally want you to experience the same pain. This lack of support has been one of the biggest problems I've seen in West Africa for the U.S. immigrant community.

At times, writing this book was very hard. It wasn't easy to detail every ordeal I've passed through to get to where I am today. Yet I hope my story will inspire individuals who find themselves in the same situation to think of executing their own future because no one else will, not even their parents or friends. As a child, I had a vision, and when my father died in March of 1993, I quickly realized that I had to assemble a toolbox of specialized tools to help me execute this vision. I don't believe in dreams, I believe in vision because unlike dreams, visions provide someone with a clear path to arriving at the desired goal.

In writing this book, I wanted to offer an honest accounting of the values I believe helped me succeed. I offer this to those who are still struggling to find their way, the way my father offered his words of wisdom to me as a teenager, and the way friends like Specialist Bradley Beard, may his soul rest in perfect peace, and George offered their wisdom to me as an adult.

Acknowledgement

When the time finally came to put my thoughts to paper, I was still not prepared to do so because I thought whatever I have to say or write wouldn't have any impact, but I will leave that to the readers. In March 2020, as every business and organization began the transition from inside offices to teleworking due to the COVID-19 pandemic, I discussed my ideas with a couple of friends and family members about writing a memoir that will chronicle my journey. They threw their support behind me, but as we may know, the start of everything seems tedious and cumbersome. I also thought that the idea of working from home could be a very good opportunity to juggle between my work and writing my memoir and a couple of months later, I saw an almost-complete book. As a tradition, at the end of every book, authors take out their time to thank people and I intend to do that here also to keep the tradition going.

First and foremost, I owe unreservedly my gratitude to God Almighty who guided me throughout my arduous travels and during the process of writing this book. I am highly favored by him and I will always bow before him to render my gratitude. Secondly, to my parents who are not here today to see who and what I have become, I dedicate this book to both of you, Mr. Lare Dambre and Mrs. Francisca Lare (Soubre) for your endless love. To my father, in African culture, children are always children and can't have a meaningful conversations with adults or parents, but this man I call father always sat me down and had conversations like friends. "Nothing good comes easy and the things that come that easy, will go easily", My father told me one day. This is what kept me and still keeps me going when the road seems tough. Daddy, I am highly indebted to you and I know you'd be proud of me for flouting the impossible. To my mother, you were my employee from the moment you conceived me to when you delivered me. I love you and thank you for the gift of life. I'd like to dedicate this book to my girlfriend, Herta Shikongo for her moral and spiritual support. She has been keeping me in check whenever I seem to slide. To Ms. Sadia Pessinaba, I am highly indebted to you for your time in reviewing many of my transcripts and pointing out the many mistakes I made. Even though we met in a very short period of time, you have been a good friend, mentor, and such an influential individual in my life. Thank you.

To my many friends, notably, Mr. Bema Yeo, your encouragement to put this book together is unparalleled. You are not only a brother, but also, we both are in the same doctoral program, and you have always been keeping me in check when things seemed very difficult and tough. Thank you, brother. You have been mentoring me and guiding me throughout this process. To you, I say thank you, and may God Almighty be at the center of everything you undertake. Love conquers all.

1

Voices from Afar

The late afternoon sun beat down on my hair as my bare, calloused feet picked their way over rocks and across grasses, careful not to step on the animal droppings left behind by the two cows I herded up every day on Nassau and Won't Mountains. As the cattle grazed on green grass, and sometimes corn or sorghum stalks, I thought about my own long finished lunch and the dinner I would need to hunt. Later that afternoon I would have to kill a hare with my catapult, then make a fire and prepare the meat with the corn and yams I'd carried up the mountain that morning.

The temperature hovered around 45°C (114°F), and the humidity hung over me. I stepped along with an eye out for rattlesnakes, vipers, and any other poisonous reptiles then ducked into one of the boulders-formed caves to escape the sun and feel the coolness of the stones for a minute. From inside the darkness of the cave, I looked down into the valley between Nassog and Won't Mountains where my village resides. Composed of five mud huts, with thatched roofs connected by mud walls, the village included a hut for my mother, a hut each for my father's first and third wives, and a hut for each of my two elder brothers.

Suddenly, a sound of voices drifted up the mountain towards me. It was my age-mates, who lived throughout the village on their return from school, singing the songs they had learned that day.

What were they *singing? What were* the *words? Why* had *they learned those songs that day?*

I should have been with them, I thought. *Learning the songs along with them.*

As I listened to their voices, I remembered the recruiters coming into my house six months before to see if I had come of age to attend school. There were very few records in the village, and many children did not even have their birth certificates or know their exact ages, so the government sent recruiters to the villages to determine school age.

Whenever they came into the house, my parents would try to hide me, because when the recruiters found a school-age kid and recorded that kid's name in the register, that kid had to go to school. My parents weren't the only ones hiding their child. Other parents in the village were hiding my age-mates, anyone, who was six or seven. These parents were hiding their kids because they didn't have money to send them to school at that time. Basically, the government was forcing parents to send kids to a school they could not afford. They couldn't pay the tuition. The recruiters would come and recruit kids, but it wasn't free. There weren't just school fees, but also the books, supplies, and food needed to go to school.

The only way the recruiters could tell the kids' age was by measuring kids with the simple test of asking them to stretch their right hand over their head and grasp their left ear. If kids could do this, they were ready for school.

I knew I was almost six years old, the age for school, but the recruiters measured my head anyway, and when my right hand reached my left ear, they concluded it was time for me to go.

They told my father, "It is time for him to go to school."

I was excited to join my older brothers and sisters at school.

Yet I had been born into a family that could barely put $.50 cents of food on the table.

Having an animal herder was the number one priority for the family. So, my father said, "No. He will remain to herd the cattle." By the way, the cattle were only 2 bulls that the family used to plow during the rainy season.

My age-mates went off to school and left me at home.

For the next month or two, I continued along with herding the family cattle. I would leave the house at 8:30 in the morning. There were other people herding their cattle in the mountains from different houses, and we were like a family, we would kill birds and eat together, but still, I wanted to go to school. In the afternoons, during the rain, I would duck into the caves for shelter, starting hesitantly, checking that no wild animal was going to lunge out at me. From the cave, I could look down at several villages spreading out below me.

The houses where we lived were made from mud. Unfortunately, when it did rain heavily, the whole mud structure would fall on the people who were sleeping at night. I remembered experiencing this once myself when I was six, sleeping in my mom's room. When it started raining, the wind came and blew off the roof, and we were just lying there, watching the rainfall in the room. We had to run out of that room and go into another room where it was safe.

From the cave, I would look over at the town of Warkambou, about six kilometers away, where my siblings and age-mates were sitting in school. I would sit in the cave, wondering what they were learning. What did they do there in school?

Every afternoon, I would hear my age-mates coming home from school, singing some songs. Kind of like *together or valor*. Singing with that special cadence.

I would be on the mountain, hearing those songs. I figured it was also time for me to go to school. Because I wanted to know what was there, what made them sing those kinds of songs.

As I led the cattle down from the mountain, I could hear my age-mates speaking up close. They were recounting some stories that were so unique. They started speaking French words, and I didn't understand what they were saying. That was the start of my jealousy.

When I got down from the mountain around 6:30 at night, I said, "Daddy and Mom, I have to go to school."

And they said, "Well, you can't go to school right now because you have to take care of the cattle. Your sisters and brothers are going, and you're the only one who can take care of them right now."

I knew that the two cows I was responsible for could not be sold for food as they were meant to plow whenever the rainy season came. Without them, we would have to wait for everyone else to finish their work before they could lend us theirs to plow. The season passed by so fast that if one was delayed when it was raining, they could fall behind and might not get crops or food to feed the family.

"Okay," I said. I agreed with them because I couldn't see any other choice, but I knew one day, I would see my chance, and I *would* go to school.

After another year of herding cattle and watching my age-mates with jealousy, I again told my parents, "I want to go to school."

And they still said, "No!"

I stood in the valley and faced the mountains, Nassog on the left, and Wona'ab on the right. All I knew was the mud houses where we lived and herding cattle in these mountains and catching birds with my catapult. I was curious and wanted to know what was in school. I wanted to go and learn more about the world and also become like my brothers and sisters, but for then, I obeyed my parents.

In September of 1986, when I was seven, almost eight, and the school year was just beginning, I decided *I* would go to school. That day I woke up in the morning and looked around. Nobody was there. My sisters, my brothers, they had all gone to school. I realized I had to take drastic measures. I thought to myself *"I am going to run out of the house and go to school."* I knew that if I took the time to dress up and put on clothes, my parents would see that I was going some*where*. So I ran out of the house naked and went to school.

When the time came to act, I didn't hesitate. I knew very well that this was the right time to make a move and defy my father's terrifying look and go to school. I didn't care if he saw me as a renegade or a disobedient child because I had an objective to achieve: going to school with my age-mates.

Now I didn't even know the route to school. It was about five to six kilometers away in the town of Warkambou, while my father lived on the outskirts of Warkambou in a tiny place called Tambisgou. I had to ask people on my way to school, "Hey, where is the location of this school?"

They would show me, and say, "Where are you going?"

And I would say, "I'm going to school."

"You go to school naked?" they asked.

"Yep."

I was able to get to school on time. Everyone was at the assembly, gathered, and starting to hoist the flag. I ran over quickly and found my oldest sister.

My poor sister. She was shy, and now her brother had come in naked, and everybody was looking at him. I could vividly see in her face that she felt like this was the end of her life. I could hear the fear in her voice when she told me, "You've just put me in trouble." We both knew our father was a little bit tough, especially when we disobeyed his commands.

Yet she grabbed me and tried to cover me.

The headmaster saw me and said, "You have to go home and put on something."

"I'm not going to go home until my name is written in that registry." I said, pointing to a large book I saw sitting on the headmaster's desk. I could not tell exactly if it was a register because I couldn't read, but I believed it was that big book. "Write that I'm ready to go to school."

"You go home and come back in your clothes and bring your slate," the headmaster said.

"Headmaster, I am not going home until you promise me that I'm going to go to school."

He looked at the three teachers—one for first and second grade, another for third and fourth grade, and another for fifth and sixth grade—and said, "You know what, we're going to have to do whatever this little boy *wants* in order to get him out of here." He picked up the book and wrote down my name.

I believed that he had written my name in the register.

My sister said, "Now, okay, let's go home and you can put on clothes and come back."

On the walk back home, I could tell my sister was a little bit frightened. Taking me back home would mean that my father would probably not allow her to take me back to school. "There's going to be a struggle," she said. "There's going to be a fight. Maybe *I* won't even be allowed to go back to school today."

As she was saying these words, I had a very clear image of my father coming toward me with his hand behind his back. That hidden hand would be holding his black belt, and he would be coming towards me to beat me. I had been beaten by him before. Corporal punishment was normal for us.

No sooner than my sister had expressed her doubts, she said, "Let's go. Let's go home and see what happens."

I gave thanks to my sister who was very courageous.

We went home, and my father came out to meet us. By now it was 8:30, the time I usually took the cattle up the mountain, and he had noticed I was not at home. In the village, parents did not worry too much about missing kids…they were usually just at home or off with their friends. They didn't believe you could just vanish. My father's attitude was, *wherever he's gone, he was going to come back.*

My father had a unique way of expressing his anger or disapproval. His eyes spoke louder than his mouth and that was how we knew we were in trouble.

My sister spoke up. "My little brother actually showed up to school naked and he made an agreement with the Headmaster that he was going home and back to school.

My father made a sound to try to clear his throat as if he wanted to speak, but he still wasn't saying anything. He taunted us with his eyes, sending us into a panic.

I thought, *Oh my God, what is going to happen to us?* I was sure he could see the fear in our eyes. I was just waiting for him to say, "You're not going back to school. Get your butt out there and take care of the cows."

But my father was quiet. I could see him thinking about it, about his son who wanted to go to school to become educated. My father knew he couldn't change the agreement I'd made with the headmaster.

Finally, he said, "As much as I would like you to go to school, if you go now, who is going to take care of the cattle?"

"Daddy," I said. "I don't know. Maybe today they'll go hungry. But I have to go back to school."

He finally noticed that I was determined to go to school, so he accepted defeat. "Okay, he said. "If you want to go to school, go." We're going to have to find a Fulani."

The Fulani are the nomad people who go from one place to another.

"We'll find someone like that to come and take care of the cattle while you go to school."

With those words, he agreed to send me back to school.

"Okay, *great!*" I said. "Daddy, thank you so much."

My sister let out a big sigh of relief. We were all excited. I ran into the house to get some clothes. Everything I had to put on was torn and raggedy, but at least they were clothes and I could go to school. No one in my family had special clothes to wear to school. We couldn't get nice pants. We didn't even have shoes to wear. My sister and I gathered up some leaves and tied them into socks and put them on our feet to protect them from the heat because the sandy paths we walked to school were burning hot. That was what we needed to do. When we walked to school, we didn't walk in the middle of the road, but single file along the edge of the road, trying to step on some leaves to cool our feet off a little bit. We knew that if we walked in the sand, we would burn our feet.

So I went to school. My sister and I walked all the way back. All those miles I was thinking about my father's face and how he must have been thinking about how much I wanted an education and how he wasn't going to stop me. I kept hearing his words, "If you want to go to school, go."

I was so excited. I finally saw the inside of the school. The structure was almost like our mud houses, except our mud houses were well built to prevent rain from coming in. The Public Primary School of Warkambou, as it was called, was made of wood and extremely poorly roofed. I already knew from my brother's and sister's experiences that, in the case of rain, there would be no classes.

The school began in first grade, so even though I was already eight, the headmaster took me straight to class 1, first grade. Even though I was a newcomer to this class, I could say most of the students were my age because most of them had repeated first grade. When I stepped in, the entire class looked at me as if they wanted to say something to me. I met my fellow schoolmates and saw my age-mates who were all there.

The teacher was well-dressed in a striped red and white shirt, with black pants, and well-polished black shoes. However, as the day went on, I noticed his shoes starting to get dusty from all the dust in the classroom. But the next day, he would be back, his shoes shined anew, ready for a new day, which again ended with his dusty shoes.

There were about 20 kids in first grade and perhaps 10 in third and fourth grades and 6 or 7 in fifth and sixth grades.

I was so determined to go to school that I listened to everything very carefully. When I would go home, I would be repeating everything I knew, not just so I would remember it, but so my parents would see that I'd learned something.

The very first week, my teacher saw something in me. When he gave us the exercise of learning the ABCs in French, I got it on the first try. He read the whole twenty-six letters, and I tried my best to retain them.

Then he said, "Okay, I've read them to you, who can read them back to me?"

One of the students stood up and started reciting, "A, B, C, D, E, F…" then he was stuck.

"David," the teacher said. "You try."

I got up and I read from A to Z. That was my first time speaking any French.

"Wow," the teacher said. "That's good. That's really, really good." After that, he said, "I'm going to make you the class Prefect."

It was funny to me that someone who just came in and didn't even know the school rules was named class Prefect.

"Have you ever been to school before?" the teacher asked me.

"No sir," I said. "It's my first time."

"Oh, wow," he said. "That is really something."

I had grown up learning my tribal language, but now that I was in school, I was going to be learning French, which was the national language. Like the songs I learned in school, learning French turned out to be very important to my career and my life's path.

I was excited when we moved on to learning those songs I had heard my age-mates singing while I was herding the cattle up on the mountain.

The first song I learned was about the military march.

Marché, marché, marché
Jolie battalion
Battalion qui marche
Oh, au son de la musique...

The battalion is marching to the rhythm of the song. We are like soldiers and we are fighting for our own lives. The idea was that the way the military marches, sings, and focuses is the same way students focus on achieving their goals.

Another song was about sickness/rich

Maladie, tu es mon ennemi
Tu me prends comme un homme riche
Je ferai tout pour t'eviter
Car prevenir vaut mieux que guerir

How am I supposed to continue with my studies?

Sickness, you know, you take me for a rich person, meanwhile, I am not rich. If you make me sick, how am I supposed to continue with my studies? I will do whatever it takes to avoid you or mitigate you.

Those kinds of songs had a specific meaning in building us to believe in something, mainly that without education your life is completely useless—education is the most important thing—but they also weren't offering any resources so we could go to school.

The school didn't even have a library. There were about five books for the whole class. We would all take turns taking one of the books. We relied on the notes we copied down from the blackboard. Whatever notes we took from the teacher was the only thing we had to study. We didn't have any additional resources where we could look up information and relied solely on the teacher.

But those songs we sang stuck with me, and I would remember them many times throughout my life. When we sang, our voices whispered of the greater world, and these whispers eventually led me out of my village.

I started school in the final semester of the year, so it wasn't long until the final exams. In the final exams that year, I came in first in my class.

Being first in a class like that, I was intimidating to the other kids, and they started to bully me. I would buy my own food to take to school, and they would take my food away, then beat me up. I couldn't tell anybody because my teachers and parents wouldn't believe me, and they would probably beat me again. So I just kept quiet. There was a real stigma about complaining about bullying in that culture, especially in those days. The adults didn't believe bullying hurt a kid but putting up with it made him a stronger person.

This bullying went on and on for almost a year. One day I decided to say, "No. This is enough. I am going to have to fight for *my*self."

I planned to wait for the boy who always took my food from me. That blessed morning, I saw him coming. I stood up and slapped him in the face. I knew I could beat him, but I was afraid that the teachers, or maybe the other students, would get crazy with me. If the teachers decided to punish me, it would be 5 to 10 lashes.

But I wasn't punished, and my tormentor left me alone. After that I was a happy boy, going to school, first in first grade. I was first in second grade. First in third, fourth, fifth, and sixth grade.

The King's Grandson

My family lived in Northern Togo, in a city called Warkambou. This city is on the border of Togo and Ghana, and we often went to Ghanaian markets on foot, and Ghanaians frequented our markets, which were held every Thursday and Sunday.

Growing up, there was no electricity. There is still no electricity as I write this book. However, I was informed by one of my siblings that the government has finally planted some electric poles, and very soon there will be lights in the streets and in homes.

The houses were very close together. In Togo, with a population of 8 million, there are forty to fifty registered languages and many more unregistered languages. Each house was speaking different languages, including Moba, Manprusi, and Kusaal.

Even though I came from this particular place, this extreme poverty, I still thought that I had a future.

My brothers and sisters were all first in their respective classes. We were doing well in our studies, but we were the poorest people at school. It was hard for my father to put five dollars of food on the table for all my family members.

This may come as a surprise because in front of the school, lived my grandfather, who was the king. On our breaks, we would visit him at his house. We would get food to eat and talk to him. Our grandfather was the most powerful king in that village.

My grandfather had married twenty-six wives. Each wife gave him no less than ten kids. Sometimes I would wonder if all the kids even belonged to him because it would be crazy to keep up with twenty-six wives. Yet in Togo, having many wives is a prestigious thing, an honor. If you're king, you marry a lot of wives and that gives you glory and makes you a more powerful king.

My father, son of the king, had married three wives. In addition to adding to a man's prestige, wives were necessary for economic reasons in this agricultural community. The more helping hands, the bigger farm a man could have and the bigger his agricultural prowess. When a man married two or three wives, his farming went faster than someone who married only one wife. Having more children was another economic factor. The more children, the bigger the farm could be. The quicker the farmer could clear his fields and grow more crops. He could do it "Biggie," as we would say.

In this farming community, land ownership was the most important component of wealth. And it still is. My father didn't have enough cattle. He had left his father's compound and gone off to build his own house. He couldn't go back and ask for money, so we struggled.

We were poor, but we had knowledge and intelligence. It didn't matter if we had food to eat, we still did well in school.

I'll never forget the day my grandfather died.

When a king dies, the family doesn't tell everyone right at once. They don't want the general public to know because they need time to name the next king.

That day, my family members told the other adults, "The king is traveling."

To us children, they said, "Your grandfather traveled, and he's going to be back."

But as the day turned to night, we began to have our doubts.

My grandfather had a symbolic lion, which symbolized his power as king. That night, when my grandfather died, the lion made a loud sound. This sound traveled to us over six kilometers away. Then we knew there was something wrong. Even though our parents wouldn't tell us, we knew because we had heard the stories about previous kings and what happened when they died. That lion's sound gave us the hint that our grandfather was no longer.

Another thing that gave us this hint that our grandfather had died was a star. It was a small, very bright star. The night that he died, my sisters and brothers were all together, telling stories. We saw this star emerge into the sky, illuminated outside the usual blue of the moon and stars, and it highlighted the whole village, like a light. It was so bright you could see everything on the floor. It was *too* bright to look at directly. It was a big star, just going down towards the horizon, the way a ball would fall back to Earth, and then, seconds later, it fell. When it fell, we heard the sound of a loud boom. We didn't know where it fell, but we heard it. Probably it was debris or something from space, but it coincided with his death, and we believed that it was his star that fell off, the way our stories told us that each person has a star and that when you die, your star falls out of the sky.

"Your Bicycle Money is in Your Stomach"

In 1992, I was in sixth grade, and because of my father delaying my school start, I was thirteen years old. Now, I faced another challenge. After sixth grade, students sit for an exam, which they must pass, in order to go to seventh grade. The exam takes about five days to write, and the exam center was in a different city, forty kilometers away from my home. In order to go there, I needed a means of transport. My father didn't have a bicycle, he didn't have a motorbike, and of course, he didn't have a car.

So far in my family, only one older brother has taken this exam. He had borrowed a bike from his friend's father.

I knew I had to go ask somebody to help me with a bike. I went to see my father's brother's son who I called my brother and was around thirty years old.

He had an old bike, all tied up. It wasn't the best, but at least I could ride it to the center.

"Brother," I said. "I need your bike. There are some exams coming up, and I need to go there and write my exams."

I was surprised by the words that came out of his mouth. He said, "Your bicycle money is in your stomach."

It felt like a slam in the face. He didn't want to loan it to me. I knew he meant that if I wanted a bike I would have to work hard, buy my own bike, and then I could go sit for my exam. Instead of doing this, he was accusing me of spending all my money on food. He didn't say it out loud, but I knew he meant: *If you don't have a bike, then you're not going for* that *exam*.

"Well," I said. "I do understand that I could have done some*thing*, but I am just a small boy, so I can't do that much. I'm trying. I'm struggling to buy my school books and my pencils. In order to get all the money to buy a bicycle, I think I have to sell myself."

"No," he said. "I'm not going to give it to you."

Meanwhile, the exam date was approaching in only two days. I had to go in search of a bicycle that I can ride to the center. I needed to go there the day before the exam so I could find a place to stay and study before the exam. Yet, I was still struggling to get a bike and couldn't study. I didn't have the stable mind a person likes to have before an exam. I couldn't eat well, sleep well, or even relax.

The day of the exam, I went to another guy who was not related to my family. I asked, "Can I borrow your bike and go write my exam?"

"When is that?" he asked.

"The exam is today actually."

"*What?*"

"Yep. It is today."

"Whoa," he said. "Where's it at?"

"It's forty kilometers away."

"Take that bike," he said. "And go write your exam."

I took the bike and set off, speeding along as fast as I could. All the roads in my village began as dirt paths from when people got up and started walking somewhere. Some of these paths had been widened into roads by people walking them. They were dirt roads and full of potholes. When I would reach a river, I would have to get off and lift the bike and carry it over my head as I waded through the water. The whole time I was crossing the river, I would be thinking how dangerous this was because I could be attacked by crocodiles or snakes. This fear wasn't helping me relax for the exam. And I still had to get to the center!

When I was across the river, I would start riding again. Halfway there, my bike tire got a puncture. There wasn't any mechanic handy so I took off the tire and tied it up with a plastic wire and inflated it with the pump I had with me. It worked! I set off again and got there two hours later.

There was a police officer stationed at the exam center, controlling who went in and out and making sure students weren't cheating by writing stuff on their palms.

I ran to the police officer and told him my story. I showed him my identity card.

"They've already finished two subjects," he said. "What are you going to do?"

"I'm going to have to sit that exam," I said. "I'm going to have to write it and see what happens. If I pass, great. If I don't, at least I know how it feels to take the exam."

He allowed me to go in.

I sat for the rest of that day, and the four days following, but I had already missed the first two parts of the exam, so no matter what I did, it was not easy to catch up. At the end of the exam, I was missing .25 points to get the grade level pass. That meant I failed that year. I had to go back to sixth grade again and repeat the whole year. That was the only year I ever had to repeat, and I blamed it on what my so-called brother did to me. If he would have loaned me his bicycle, I would have passed that exam.

Sometimes, our enemies are in the family because this brother of mine who refused to give me the bike wanted my failure and wanted me to ultimately drop out as he did himself. But the guy outside my family, who helped me, had no interest in my failure, but rather wanted my success.

Before I had to go back to the exam center to retake the exam the next year, I made sure I had my own bike.

Throughout my childhood, I'd been cultivating my own crops, like peanuts, rice, and beans. I would harvest two bags of rice or peanuts, wait until the price went up, and then I would sell them at the market. During the school year, I would buy candies, and on our break, I would sell them to the other students.

I would not make a lot of money, but this is how I'd gotten the money to pay for my school books, my own clothes, and food. My father had so many children that he couldn't buy everything for everybody. We had to fend for ourselves.

Now I was fourteen, retaking my sixth-grade year, and I was saving my money to buy a bicycle. We did not have a bank where I lived. If I put my money down, and someone else saw it—my mom, my brother, my half-brother—they would take it. So, when I sold my crops or the candies at school, I would take that money and dig a hole, wrap the paper money in a piece of cloth, and bury it. I was the only person who knew where to retrieve that money. I didn't tell anyone else about it, because I knew if I did, they would take it.

I sold and saved and buried my money for almost a year. As we were getting close to the exam time I counted my money and I had 50,000 Franc CFA. Fifty thousand Franc CFA is the equivalent of $40-45 US dollars.

I went to my direct elder brother and said, "Hey, I want to go buy a bike. A *secondhand* one."

He looked at me puzzled, and said, "Where did you get the money from?"

"Well, I have the money."

"Where? Show me the money."

"I am not going to show you the money until we see the bike. Then I will show you." I knew that if I showed him now, he was probably going to snatch the money from me, and he was going to spend it. "I want you to tell me where I can buy a secondhand bike."

"Okay," my brother said. "We are going to go to the market."

Before we went to the market, I went behind the house and dug my money from the hole. When I returned, I didn't unwrap the money from the cloth, but I held it up and showed it to my brother. "Here is the money. It is enough for a secondhand bike."

We walked to the market and found the area where a man was selling second-hand bikes.

I looked through the bikes and found a bike I liked—it was the Phoenix model—that I thought I could afford. As was usual in our markets, there was no price tag. Nothing was ever marked with a price tag; you had to bargain for a price.

"I would like to get this bike," I said.

"Well, this is 60,000," the owner said.

I only have 50,000, I was thinking. *Where are we going to get the extra 10,000?*

My brother looked at me and said, "Do you have 60,000?"

"No. I only have 45,000." I didn't tell my brother about the other 5,000 because it would help me to buy some other stuff I needed. I told the guy, "Hey, we have only 35,000."

He looked at us like we were crazy to jump from 60,000 to 35,000, but he said, "It's okay. You know we can work together. What is your final price?"

"My final price is 35,000."

"Look, son, if you want to buy this bicycle, you'll have to go up a little bit. At least go to 50,000. If you give me 50,000, I will take it."

My brother got my attention. "Tell him we have 50,000."

"Stop," I said. "We don't have 50,000. We only have 45,000."

"If it's only 45,000, I can't sell it to you." The vendor wanted to leave. He moved to take the bike away.

"Okay," I said. "If you're going to take it, take it."

"Look," my brother said to me, shaking his finger at me. "Next time, don't take me to go buy something that you don't have enough money for."

I brushed off my brother's comments.

We turned our backs to walk away. Then I heard the seller yell, "Hey guys, come back, come back, come back." I looked over my shoulder and saw him waving his hand at us. "Come back again. Okay, I'll give it to you guys for 45,000."

"You see," I told my brother, a big grin on my face. "We got the price we wanted for the bike." I drove my fist into my other hand to emphasize this victory.

"Good," my brother said.

Now, I had a bike, and my brother had a bike. We had a bike in the family. We were all happy. If someone got sick, we could ride that person to the dispensary.

Now that I had my bike, I went back to the exam center and took my exam. I passed, first in my class, which completed my primary schooling. I went on to seventh grade, and college schooling, at the Collège d'Enseignement Générale (CEG) de Lotogou, about 2 kilometers away from my village.

Before school started, everybody knew about me. Students and teachers alike would hear about me, things like, "This guy is very brilliant. Very intelligent."

When I got there, I would hear people saying, "Hey, is that that boy they've been talking about? Is that the guy? We will challenge him because this is not primary school, this is college. College is a little different."

But it didn't matter that the classes were harder.

There was one teacher who said, "In my class, no one can score 15/20 on this essay."

But the first essay question he gave us, I scored 19/20. He was surprised and shocked.

I came in first in my seventh-grade classes.

That Fateful Day of My Father's Death

The structure of the family was that there was a mud fence around the houses. Men would stay outside the fence and would put up tents outside under the trees. The men would be sitting outside, and the women would be inside the house, cooking. After they finished cooking, they would come and ask us, boys and men, if we wanted to go inside to eat or if they should bring the goods outside so we can all eat. After we ate, the women would come back outside and pick up our plates.

My father was one of the best guys, of course every child would say, but I really mean this deep from my heart. I thought he was the best father. Even though I didn't like it when I was young and he wouldn't let me go to school, after that, he and I would speak as friends. My father had three wives. My mother was the second wife, and I was the youngest of her five children. His first wife had six children, and the third wife had another six.

Of all seventeen children, my father wouldn't call any other child to speak with him, the way he called me. He would sit me down and say, "Hey, son, life is not what you see. All the good things come with trials."

He would tell me about getting a wife. "If you want to get a good wife," he would tell me. "You have to *work* for it. You have to go and *look*. Any good wife is hard to come by. Therefore, it is up to you to get out there and *fight* for what belongs to you."

I saw his words as an opportunity to move past the picture of my wife and see whether this idea was something I could deploy in the future in any field. That was who I *was*, even as a little boy. I was different from my siblings. Everything that my siblings were doing, I was completely different. I would do the opposite. When they went to the left, I would go to the right. When they went to the right, I would go to the *left*. My parents were so frustrated that their little boy was acting this way.

My father would sit me down and talk to me like a brother, like a friend.

"Daddy," I would say. "Why are you telling me all this?" He could have been talking to any of my elder brothers or sisters. "I'm just a boy. I don't know anything yet."

"I sense something in you," he said. "I know what I'm telling you, you can use it in the future."

As a son of a king, my father had some responsibilities. My grandfather would call him and send him to meetings. My father went to school through sixth grade, and he could speak Spanish, English, and many diverse languages.

I used to wonder how he learned so many languages. I think maybe I got my genes from him.

After my grandfather died, a successor wasn't named because there was infighting in the family about who would succeed my grandfather. For a time, my grandfather's first son took over, but that arrangement didn't last because he died. My father was supporting the chieftain duties and was a political leader in our constituency. He had been named the leader of a particular political party in our area because in the past my grandfather always sent him to meetings, and everyone knew him. By this point, my father had a motorbike, which had been given to him in the course of a political campaign.

My father would call me and say, "Hey, I want to go to a meeting. I want you to take me there."

Whenever he wanted to go to a meeting, he would say, "Hey, son. I want you to take me to this place. I don't want anybody else. I want *you* to take me to the meeting."

Whenever he asked, I took him to the meetings.

One day in the middle of the rainy season, it rained really hard. He wanted me to take him to a meeting. I said, "Daddy, it has rained and the road is not good. You're going to have to sit really still on the back. If you don't sit up straight…well, the road is a little bit tricky."

"Son, are you ready?"

"Yep daddy!"

"Okay, let's go."

He sat on the back and held my shoulders. I was about to start the motor. But I got distracted and pressed on the gas too hard. The front of the motorbike lifted up into the air, and we fell down into the mud.

My father stood up, trying to wipe the mud from his hands, and said, "Son, look, I'm not going to blame you. I know you probably think I'm going to slap you or beat you up for dropping me in the mud, but it's okay. Maybe there is a *reason* why we fell down. I want you to go. I am not going to go by myself. I want you to take the motorbike and go tell them that I'm not going to be able to make it."

As I rode the motorbike to the meeting, I thought about that cool side of my father, that human side. Regardless of the struggle, we went through, that human part of him was what made me *love* him so much.

When I arrived at the meeting, it was going along well. The meeting was about land ownership. They were trying to appropriate land for different kings and different villages so they could begin to farm. Some people felt that they were not given a fair share of the appropriation of the land. As I watched, some people became very agitated, and a fight broke out. Everybody was just slapping each other, punching each other's faces. It turned into a huge brawl.

When I saw that brawl, I wanted to let the person who was leading the meeting know that my father was not coming. My only goal was to get to that person and tell him why my father didn't show up, so they didn't use that against him. I was able to get close and tell him. After that, I had to leave because the way that fight was going, I was just a small boy, and there was no way I could fight anybody. I had to protect myself so I ran out.

I rode the motorbike back home and told my father what had happened there.

"You see what I told you?" he said. "Everything happens for a reason. Probably if I would have gone, I would have been killed. Or I would have gotten involved in that fight, and it would not be *good*. So everything happens for a reason."

That was the day I became a *believer* in fate. I thought: *If you are going to a place and something happens to stop you, don't go. Go back and stay home. Because if you go, something bad is going to happen.*

If we had been Christians then, we would have called it the Holy Spirit. But we were not Christian then, nor were we Muslim. We had no religious beliefs. We just believed in the deities.

My father was the kind of person who would give me advice on life and explain how life worked.

In early January 1993, when I was fifteen, he pulled me aside and started a conversation that still strikes me today.

"Son," he said. "I want you to take care of the family."

I sat there, trying to understand his words. *You* want *me to take care of the family*? How do you want me to take care of the family? Meanwhile, I have my big brothers who are already doing their part to take care of the family. Finally, I asked, "How do you want *me* to take care of the family?"

He repeated his words in a very matter-of-fact tone. "I want you to take care of the family. Because I've seen that *you* have something specific that I don't understand. I don't know what it is, but I want you to take care of the family." He nodded his head to emphasize his words. "When I'm no longer here."

I agreed reluctantly because I knew nothing of what he was expecting of me. In order to make him happy, I said, "Father, I will take care of the family the way you want me to."

In January of 1993, he fell sick.

I had a sinking feeling inside me when I remembered our conversation of the month before. He had made all those statements about him wanting me to take care of the family because he saw the end was coming.

His sickness was something that nobody could understand. He could not speak. When he tried to speak, he couldn't make any complete sentences. He could only make short, incoherent statements.

I kept asking myself, *what* is *he saying*?

Then he would laugh or smile.

"Daddy?" I asked. "What is going on?"

This kind of exchange would happen off and on, so I didn't see the urgency of the situation. I didn't think this sickness was something serious that was going to lead to death. We didn't have any hospitals near us. We had something called dispensaries where we could get aspirin or Tylenol for headaches or Band-Aids when we cut our fingers. There was no medical center that diagnosed conditions.

Traditional healers came in and considered what might be wrong with him and then used herbs to treat him. They boiled herbs for him to drink. Nothing they did seemed to improve his condition.

As the weeks went by, my father continued speaking incoherently.

"Daddy?" I asked the man who always gave me advice. "What *is* going on?"

I was still hoping he would go back to giving me the answers, but he could not say what was going on with him.

When he could not speak, he smiled.

When he did make statements, they made no sense.

This pattern continued for nearly a month.

I started to feel more and more worried. *This is serious*, I thought.

By March, he couldn't utter any more words. He could not get up. He was just paralyzed. He could no longer do anything.

Whoa, I thought. I was really starting to understand what he'd been telling me when he told me to take care of the family when he was no longer.

On March 8 of 1993, my father finally looked into my eyes and said, "I'm going." That was the last time my father spoke. That fateful day my father died at 3 PM.

After my grandfather had died, five years earlier, nobody took over as king. Initially, my uncle, who was my grandfather's first son, took over, but there is a general theory about legends. When a living legend dies, their children cannot live up to that level.

I know without a doubt that my father should have taken over, but because of politics, he didn't. My father was the one who was running the errands for my grandfather. He was well known to everybody in the kinship circles. He was very well known to the president of Togo. When my grandfather died, *he* was supposed to take over. Even though my grandfather hadn't started this, it was apparent because of my father's exposure to the duties of a king.

Some of us suspect that my father's death could have been caused by the fact that he was in line to become the king. We think that they killed my father in order to get the kingship. The kingship entirely broke down, and the family couldn't get the kingship any longer. It became political. Rumor has it that he was poisoned by one of his brothers who thought my father was going to be the next king, so they wanted to get him out of the way.

There is no longer a king in my village, but the power is held by an elected official. They no longer follow the tradition of kings that go along the family tree.

My father was a generous person. He would give everything that he had to other people, then say to us, "Well, let people eat. When you give food to people, one day someone else is going to give it to you."

This may not come back to you directly but to your grandchildren or even your great-grandchildren.

My father said, "It is good to always give out to people. Share whatever you have with people, and you're going to be blessed. Somebody else will bless you wherever you go."

2

My Year as a Slave

Eighth Grade Dropout

Every father wants the best for his child, and my father had been preparing me for any eventuality. When he died, even though he didn't have that much money to take care of me and my financial needs, he had been a figure in the house. That was enough for me.

I was cultivating my own rice and beans so I could buy my own stuff, but the encouragement my father gave me and the times he would say, "Look, I'm here for you. You go to school," meant a lot to me. He saw the potential for my life and his encouragement carried me after his death.

When he died, I was in my final semester of seventh grade, and the weight of what he had been saying to me over the last several months about taking care of the family was weighing heavily on me. I was thinking, *okay, I'm going to school, but technically I don't have anything. My mother doesn't have money. My brothers don't have any money. My half-mothers didn't have any money. Me going to school right now doesn't make any sense. It means that I will be working part-time and won't be able to make the money I could be working full-time. Then I could take care of the family.*

So I had to decide whether to keep on going to school or leave school.

I had been wanting to go into the military ever since I was little. I saw men in uniforms, and I wondered *what makes them different from people who don't wear uniforms?*

I tried a couple of times to join the military, but it didn't work. When I presented myself, the officials said, "You can't go until you're eighteen."

Around this time, towards the end of 1994, when I was in the first semester of eighth grade, a man from my village, who I called "brother," came home for a visit. He had traveled to Ghana and came back with nice stuff, beautiful things. His hands were clean, and he was smelling of a sweet cologne.

We started talking, and he said, "Hey, look at what you're wearing. Your clothes are all torn up. If you want to go to Ghana with me and make some money, I will take you. You will come back looking like I do now."

"Wow," I said, looking again at his colorful clothes and down at my ripped-up shorts. "This is interesting." I didn't have to think about it. I make decisions like that, without dragging my feet. I make them in a split second. I think that's how I was born. "Okay," I told him. "I will go. Count me in."

"Really?"

"Yep."

"Okay, I'm leaving in three days' time."

"I'm ready," I said.

During those three days, I didn't tell anybody that I was leaving. I didn't tell my mother. None of my brothers knew. My teachers, my schoolmates, my friends, nobody knew I was going to leave. That's how I am. I don't tell people my business.

Leaving for Ghana

We had a class exam on Monday and were supposed to receive the results on Wednesday. That Wednesday I didn't show up to school. I never learned my score from that eighth-grade exam that I took. That Wednesday I packed my so-called "stuff." I filled a bag with my old, raggedy clothes and went to the brother who was going to take me to Ghana.

I spent that night at his house, along with four friends from other villages, so we could get up as early as 3 AM to start off on our journey to Ghana. We didn't have clocks but were told the time by the sound of roosters. I was so excited and on edge to see where we were going. All I could think about was getting rich and coming home wearing nice clothes and cologne. I felt like I didn't sleep at all, but I must have finally fallen asleep because I woke to the sound of a rooster.

"It's time to go!" I said, starting to jump up and grab my bag.

"It's only 1:00 am," my brother mumbled. "Go back to sleep."

I lay awake a long time, then must have fallen asleep again because then another rooster cried and woke me.

"Is it time to go?" I asked.

"It's 3:00 am," my brother said. "Let's go."

We all got up and started walking across the border to Ghana. We were walking, walking, walking. It was a seriously long walk. We crossed the river. It was the rainy season which made the river very high and risky to cross. Even though we'd prayed, and it hadn't rained in our village, it had rained upriver from us and the basin was overflowing. We know how to swim because we're in the water all the time.

My brother said, "Let's go quick. Let's run. Let's run. If we don't run this water is going to rise even higher."

We got into that river and started walking across. We held hands in a human chain, so nobody fell behind. We carried our bags on our heads.

We finished crossing that river, then looked back and gave thanks to God. We put our palms together and said, "Thank you so much for taking us across the river."

We were so excited. Me and the other three boys were all so excited we were going to Ghana, and we would return home looking like my brother. We would be wearing nice cologne and nice clothes. Everyone would look up to us the way we had looked up to my brother.

Around 11:00 am we stopped for a rest. We found some food, we ate, then we continued along.

Around 4:00 pm, we reached a point where we could no longer walk but had to take a bus across the cities and go to other villages. We didn't have any money, so our brother who was taking us had to pay for us to ride. I knew that his paying for me meant that after I worked, I would have to pay him.

"It's okay," we all told him. "When we get there, we're going to work, and then we'll pay you."

At the bus station, my brother said, "Everything I do, follow my lead. Follow my instructions. Do not do anything stupid."

"Okay," we all agreed.

I boarded the bus, and it was the first time I'd been in any type of car. Music was playing. That was something, a new experience. I was feeling big. And so excited.

This good feeling was put into perspective when my brother reminded us of the conflict that had been brewing in Northern Ghana in late 1994 between two ethnic groups: Manprusi and Dagomba. We were of the Manprusi group, with half of us settled in Togo and the other half in Ghana, and we shared the same culture. If we're lucky enough and we meet our ethnic group, we will be safe. But if we were to meet the Dagomba group, they probably would kill us because we were the enemy.

We didn't have ID cards, like in Hotel Rwanda, a film made about this ethnic conflict. The only test was if you could speak the language. If you opened your mouth, and the right words came out, they would let you pass. If the right words didn't come out, we would be their enemies, and they were going to kill us.

The bus pulled into a checkpoint.

The officials said, "Come out, come out, come out."

We stepped off the bus.

Luckily for us, they started speaking Manprusi, which was our ethnic group.

We spoke back in the Manprusi language.

"Oh, okay," they said. "Where are you guys from?"

We said, "We're from Togo, the side of Manprusi people. We're coming here to farm and earn some money for our parents."

"Okay," they said. "You'd better be careful as you go. You may meet another group of people, the Dagombas. These are bad people. They will kill you guys."

"Okay," we said, and all nodded solemnly.

Then they told the driver to take a particular route so as not to meet the Dagomba.

The driver listened, and we took the safe path.

The four of us on the bus didn't have the wherewithal to ask our brother, "What kind of job will we do that is going to give us that much money?" We were afraid to ask. I thought that if we asked too many questions he might get upset and throw us off the bus and not take us, so we just kept quiet and went.

After twelve hours on that bus, we reached the city of Kumasi, the second-largest city in Ghana. Kumasi is the capital city of the Ashanti Region, in almost-central Ghana. The Ashanti are the people that we're going to work for.

I was looking all around. The city of Kumasi was beautiful. There were beautiful houses. The roads were all well paved. There were people baking bread along the roadside. I saw many things I'd never seen where I came from. I had never seen so many cars or people selling stuff. There were stores everywhere. It was beautiful. Life seemed much more sophisticated here than where I came from. It was the most beautiful thing I'd seen in my life up until that point.

This is where I'm going to be, I thought. I was so excited. I didn't know yet that I wasn't going to stay in this beautiful place. It was a chance to see the other side of life, a glimpse of a fantasy world before we had to go to real life.

We stayed in Kumasi for one day. We didn't get a place to stay but slept at the bus station.

The next day we moved on to the village where my brother lived. "I've brought you guys here," he said. "Because there are people who are waiting for us, people who will hire you. And your bosses have paid for your bus fare. These people will take you to work on their farms."

"Farming?" one of the other boys who had traveled with us asked.

"Yes. Farming," my brother said.

The boy looked down, disgusted to discover that this was the kind of work we would be doing.

"Myself, I'm running a cacao farm in this village," my brother said.

Like that boy, I was also surprised to learn our work would be farming. My brother's hands had been so clean that I wouldn't have thought he was farming, but working in an office. That's where I thought he might be taking us, to an office where we would all work.

My brother, our leader, said, "Look guys, where you're going is going to be hard, but remember why you're here. You're here to make money to take back to your families. Whatever these people say, you'd better listen to them. If you don't listen to them, they're going to kick you out. And if they kick you out, that means you're not going to get the money. Right here you don't have any other family. I'm the only one, but guess what, I am not going to come to your rescue. So, you'd better listen to them and do what they want you to do."

"Okay," we all nodded. "We'll do that."

It was early in the morning and as four young men, we stood there. The people who came to meet us came early as well.

We all sat down on a bench, and the Ashantis who were there to buy us sat down too, like in a family meeting.

"Okay," my brother said, starting the proceedings. "This guy here," he indicated to me, the first guy sitting on the bench. "This guy has a college degree. He went to school and speaks good French. He can speak a little bit of English. He may understand what you say, but he cannot really have a conversation with you in your language."

The Ashanti language is Twi or Akan and the proceedings were conducted in this language. I would catch little bits and pieces, especially if they switched over to English. Even though I cannot speak this language, the farmers don't really care.

Because I speak French, a little bit of English, and I'm educated, my price would be a little bit higher than that of the other guys who speak fewer languages and have less schooling.

The price my brother and the farmer agreed to was 50,000 Ghanaian Cedis. To convert that into current US dollars, it would amount to no more than $50.

We didn't know how much these people had paid for us to come or how much the bus fare was. We didn't ask because the fear of asking too many questions could raise eyebrows that we're trying to know too much. I think the bus fare was 20,000 Cedis. The bosses had paid my brother, and he didn't tell us this amount. I was sitting there thinking, they're paying me 50,000, so maybe the real cost is 60,000 to 70,000, and my brother is getting the rest to pay for the bus.

"Look, Yaw, as I was called," my brother said. "You are going to go with this man."

This older Ghanaian man's name was Mr. Appau.

"You will go with him, and the 50,000 cedis will be paid to you at the end of twelve months. You will work for him and stay in his house for one year. After that, he'll give you that money, and you'll be a rich man.

"Okay," I said. But I was trying to take all this in, the type of work I would be doing and the length of time I'd be there. I hadn't thought it would be *twelve* months. I had been thinking for six months, at the most, then I would take the money back to my mother and go back to school.

Another boy went for 40,000 cedis, and the other three for 35,000 cedis. That's all I know about their stories.

I clapped my hands together. "Okay," I said. "Let's go." I thought I was going to make a lot of money. 50,000 cedis was a huge amount of money. For one year, it was a lot. I had never seen so much money.

Mr. Appau started calling me "son" and told me to call him "father." Technically, he was now my father, and I was his son. He must have been almost seventy years old, but I could tell he was very strong. I didn't have any choice but to call him "Pappa." That was what I had to call him. When he asked me to call him Pappa, I was thinking, *this guy can't really be my father*. My father has meant so much to me, and it's only possible to have one father. You can't have two fathers.

"Son," he said. "Let's go to my house in the city. I want to introduce you to my family, my daughters, and my sons. I will show them I have a new son who is an addition to the family."

"Okay," I agreed.

I said goodbye to my brother, packed my stuff, and followed Mr. Appau. We went back to Kumasi and stayed in the city for the next three days. I stayed in his beautiful house.

The Ashanti people are very good at building beautiful houses. It's well known that the Ashanti people have gold. I just looked up at this building made of cement and a façade of brick. It was so beautiful. It was a six-bedroom house. The kitchen had a refrigerator. There were big TVs in many rooms. The floor was well cemented. The rooms were air-conditioned. Everything was in that house. Every room had a square window that could be opened to look outside.

One day, I'm going to have a house like this, I thought.

His children were mostly older than me. The eldest son was forty years old, and the youngest, a daughter, was twelve. They welcomed me and asked if I could speak English.

I made the gesture for "little bit" and said, "A little." That was my communication with Mr. Appau's children. I could not speak any Twi.

Mr. Appau seemed like a nice man, a caring father. He treated me like his son.

After we left Mr. Appau's beautiful house in Kumasi, my real life was about to start. Together, we left the city on the morning of the third day and traveled first by train and then by bus.

"What day were you born?" the old man asked.

"I was born on a Thursday."

"Okay, then, in Twi, if you're born on Thursday, we will call you Yaw."

He did not call me David, but Yaw. After that, to everyone we met, he introduced me as Yaw.

The bus left us off a mile from the village of Wassa, which was not reachable by car because it was a swamp. We walked the rest of the way and reached Wassa in Western Region that evening. Smaller than a village, the houses in Wassa are cottages made of bamboo and raffia. They reminded me very much of my village, where I came from. After three days in that beautiful house in Kumasi, I wondered how I could be back in the same set of living conditions from which I set out.

What is happening here? I asked myself.

From this small village, we walked on to the old man's farm, where the structures were the same type I had known all my life. Later, I would find out that part of my job was to weave bamboo and raffia to maintain the houses.

After the cottage, the next thing I saw was Mr. Appau's farm, which was very vast, about 12 acres. The farm consisted of palm trees, pineapple trees, cassava plants, banana trees, and plantain trees.

I looked around and thought, *this is where I'm going to be working. That's a big, big farm. It has everything, every fruit. I'm not going to go hungry anymore. Wow, this is the biggest farm I've ever seen. It's beautiful.*

The first morning the old man said, "Okay, son, this is where our work is going to begin." He handed me a cutlass. "This is your machete."

For the next twelve months, that machete was an extension of my arm. I had to sharpen it really well because that's what I was going to use to weed the farm and protect myself from snakes. In addition to the machete, he gave me a pair of Wellington boots that came up to my knees because that land was watery wherever I would go. Basically, it was a swamp.

"Okay, son, this is where we're going to start."

He told me the house rules, ticking them off on his fingers. "You'll get up at 5:00 am. You'll sharpen both of our machetes. Then you'll weed around all the palm trees."

I would learn to put his machete aside. He wasn't going to start at 5:00 am. He was the boss and he was going to start around 8:00 am. Me, I'll be out there clearing undergrowth from 5:30 am. I will be out there working until he comes along and joins me, then we will work together clearing new areas to plant new trees and grow corn. He doesn't do much clearing. He mostly is there for conversation.

My father had told me wise things that this guy would never tell me and these deep conversations I had had with my father were never possible with Mr. Appau. I called him Pappa because my brother told me to do so, "Do whatever you have to do to get your money and get out." So, I thought, *I'll call him Pappa, and at the end of the year, I'll get my money.*

The only difference was that even though I called my father Daddy or Pappa, in our tribal language the word we used was "N'saam." We barely even knew our father's real name and mentioning it would be the most disrespectful thing a kid could do to his father. So it was N'saam that I said every time I addressed my father. This difference between the words Pappa and N'saam learned a small distinction between what I called Mr. Appau and my real father.

The other thing I would call him was "old man," which showed respect to him as an elder.

The first morning I started using the machete, my palms started hurting. *How can I work like this for a* whole year? I wondered. *Twelve months.* These thoughts were going through my mind. As I looked around, it was scary. There were no other houses in view. The farm was surrounded by thick, dense forests. The plantain and palm trees looked so weird, so scary.

I felt disoriented being in the thick forest, only he and I. I thought, *what if something happens here, who is going to help me?* In my home village, there were so many people around. I could just walk across the compound and see somebody I knew. In this village, there was no one.

Not to mention, we practically lived with animals. There were antelopes in the forest and crocodiles and snakes beneath my feet in the swampy water. That was why the old man gave me those boots.

The facts of my situation started to add up. All the things my brother didn't tell me when he told me he could get me a job in Ghana, and I could return looking like him. He hadn't even told me what type of work he was doing. His hands, when I saw him, looked beautiful, so I didn't know he was farming a cacao farm but maybe had some kind of office job. I thought that was what he was taking me to. I didn't expect to wind up on a farm. Now I knew he'd just taken time off before he went back to Togo and that's why his hands looked so nice.

He didn't tell me about the kind of treatment I was going to face there. Looking around, I had a cultural shock. *This is where you want me to work?* He didn't tell me I was going to be working for one year.

Each morning, as I walked to the farm, I chopped the undergrowth with my machete. I would start at the top, then chop my way down, until I could see what was underfoot. I would pile all this brush into a big pile and then we would burn it. It was a slash and burn technique. Once an area was cleared, we would plant more palm trees. The old man was very interested in planting palm trees because this tree gives so much stuff to sell.

First off, there is the fruit. All those pineapples, bananas, and plantains I saw that I thought I could eat to starve off my hunger? Guess what? The old man did not want me to eat them.

I could not get anything to eat before I went out to the fields at 5:30 am so usually I would chop the undergrowth around the trees to help them grow well, then take some fruit and eat it.

One day the old man saw me eating some bananas.

"Hey," he said. "You cannot eat that fruit. If you eat it, I'm going to take it out of your paycheck."

But I didn't care. I was too hungry to care, and I would eat it anyway, but I would take a look around first and try to eat it when he wasn't looking.

We would gather all his precious fruits and carry them on our heads to the road where the bus came by, and the bus would take them to the city and sell it and bring back the money.

In addition to the fruits, the fallen palm tree gives palm wine, which I would learn about later. Finally, the fruit gives you palm oil from which palm kernel oil can be extracted.

We planted in such a way that the trees were staggered in a triangle pattern that I laid out with a tape measure, and it all looked very beautiful.

As my brother had told me, I wasn't going to get my 50,000 cedis right away. I just worked with the old man from morning until whatever time he wanted me to on his farm.

I began to learn that he had somebody working there before me. When that person left, he had come for me. He always had somebody helping him run that farm.

It was the only two of us. There was no conversation. The only thing we heard was the noise of birds and wild animals.

This guy made a lot of money from that farm. But for me, I was living with nothing, and his treatment of me was terrible.

Because there was nobody to talk to, I would start thinking back on the conversations I had with my father before he died. I would weed those palm trees and think about what he would say if he could see me. I think he would say, "It doesn't really matter what you do, as long as you do something to take care of the family." I knew it would hurt him that I was working for someone who was mistreating me and not giving me food to eat when I was hungry and making me work all the time. He didn't let me eat food at the beginning of my stay there. He was trying to see how I was going to react to his command. Working under him, it was imperative for me to not only respect, but obey his commands, and to understand that I was under his supervision and under his care. Anything he said, stood. He tested me on that front by not letting me eat.

I was able to capture that fast and know that if he said not to eat that doesn't just mean I can't eat, it means there are many other things I can't do. It's bigger than food. I know that if I want to cut some produce and sell it, I cannot do it. I cannot do a big thing for myself. Not letting me eat was my warning from him. It was my initiation to understanding how he was going to operate.

My father would be rolling over in his grave and thinking, *I didn't see this coming, that my son would be working for someone like this and that the person would be treating him so badly.*

I knew he would be proud of me for working and taking money home for the family, but it would be hard for him to accept that I was working as a slave.

The first time the old man called me "son," I liked it, but once he started acting erratically and treating me badly, the word cut through me. I was *not* his son. But I had to put up with this or I wouldn't get my money. In my heart, I didn't want him to call me that, and I didn't want to call him my father. My father would not deprive me of eating. My father would not deprive me of making friends.

The old man told me, "You cannot make friends."

His idea was that if I made friends, then they would tell me things he didn't want me to know, maybe some stories about him. That would awaken me and make me aware of what was happening around the house. They might give me tips on how to run away or steal stuff and make my own money behind his back. I could sell his palm wine and undercut him and save the money for myself. But I didn't do that. I worked with him in all honesty.

I was an enterprising kid but working for someone else was hard when I didn't see the reward for all my labor.

Yet I was afraid of the old man going back to my brother and telling him I was a bad person, or a bad boy, a bad kid, and that story would get back to my village, to my mother. I was very afraid of that and knew it would break her heart. For my mother, I was willing to keep working.

"Out Here We Sleep with Snakes"

The structures where we slept were made of bamboo and mud. Believe me or not, those structures resembled the village structures where I was born. At night, you simply didn't need a torchlight, or a lamp to see inside because there are spaces between the mud and the bamboo through which the moonlight comes in. These spaces presented great opportunities for snakes, scorpions, and soldier ants to come in uninvited. And because I always woke up around 0530, there was no time to cook anything. However, my old man, as I had always called him, woke up around 0800. Instead of the old man cooking food and bringing it to me, he asked me to cook food in the field. I would build a fire right there and roast sweet potato or cassava, which we would eat with some plucked bananas, plantains, or pineapples.

When we went home at the end of the workday, we dug more cassava and boiled it, and smashed it with a full-size mortar and pestle. If he was in a good mood that day, he would say, "Let me help you do this." He would flip the cassava, while I pounded it with the pestle. But if he was not in a good mood, I would be holding the pestle with one hand and using the other hand to turn the cassava until it became starchy, and we could eat it.

I would also make a palm nut soup. When we felled palm trees, we would cut the neck of the palm tree. For the next two to three weeks, we would let it rot. We would leave it like that until maggots would develop on the neck.

Those maggots are really nutritious, so we extracted them and used them to prepare the soup. Mushrooms also grew from that palm tree neck, and if we didn't have meat, we would prepare the soup from mushrooms. If we had meat, like antelopes, we would add it. This soup was really good.

I climbed the palm tree with my bare feet, stepping up the trunk with a rope looped around my waist and around the tree trunk. When I wanted to go up, I'd lift up the rope and move it up at the same time as I moved my body up.

The trees were full of snakes, spiders, scorpions, and soldier ants.

One day I climbed the palm tree to get the nuts, and as I was up there, cutting off branches so I could reach the palm nuts, I saw a big, big viper staring right out at me. I knew this was a very dangerous, poisonous snake. I screamed. *Lord have mercy.* I pulled away as far as I could, and in my fear, I dropped my machete to the ground. I wanted to fall back, but I was inside the rope, and I couldn't. The rope was attached to my waist, so if I jumped, I would hurt my waist. That would be my end. But the snake was watching me, and I was watching the snake. I could sense that it was scared, just like I was scared. It didn't want to bite me, but it had to defend itself. We both held still, staring at each other. I had to go down the rope, passing in front of the snake. I thought if I were to turn my body at all, the snake would think I was coming to kill it, and it would bite me. I didn't have any good choices. If I had my machete, I could hit the snake with it, but my machete lay on the ground. If I tried to reposition myself and hit it with my hand, it would be too dangerous.

I was shaking and had only a split second to decide. I was certain this was going to be my end, either through a snake bite or falling and breaking my back. I was just helpless.

Just then, I saw the old man coming.

"Hey, Papa," I cried down. "There's a snake looking at me. I'm looking at him. The way I am, I'm stuck. If I go straight down, our faces will meet, and he'll bite me. I don't know what to do."

My boss said, "Out here we sleep with snakes. Snakes are all over. It's not going to bite you. Do whatever you need to do to get out of there and come back to work."

I was hurt by his blasé attitude. *Wow*, I thought. *Really? Okay, I'm getting the picture now.* I nodded my head. *I'm getting a really good picture.*

I had been bitten by a snake before, so I knew how it felt. When I was growing my crops back in Togo, I would uproot the peanuts, let them dry for a few days, then separate the nuts from the roots. When I gathered the dried plants up, a snake was underneath the pile, and it bit my finger. That was the worst feeling. Because we didn't have medical supplies, I was given a black stone, which is a type of magnet held up to the snake bite to suck the poison out, but it didn't work perfectly. After that the healer had me collect my urine and put it on the snake bite, then he tied my arm with a tourniquet. The healer told me, "don't sleep." His thinking was that if a person sleeps at night after a snake bite, the poison will go into the person's head and blind him. That night I didn't sleep, because whenever I would doze off, the healer would hit my head, and I would wake up. After experiencing that pain, I never wanted to be bitten by a snake again.

It really hurt me that my boss cared so little about me.

I've been bitten by a snake before, and I know how painful that is. And you just don't care.

I was able to maneuver down, down, down past the snake. I kept as much distance from it as I could, and it didn't move either. When my feet touched the ground, I was so happy. I got off the rope. I didn't get palm nuts from that tree that day. I got them from a different tree. I got them and went home.

"Hey," I said to the old man. "Maybe you could get me a ladder to climb the trees. So I don't have to get so close to a snake again. Or if I see one, I can climb down quickly."

But he didn't care. "Nope. What I want you to do, you gotta do it."

I didn't say anything more because I remembered what my brother told me before we met the Ashantis. *Do not say anything to your boss because that's your boss. If you say anything like that, you are going to be in trouble. He's not going to pay you.*

Mr. Appau's lack of caring really struck me though. I thought *wow, this is how this man wants to deal with me. I don't have any choice. I just have to do what he wants me to do, and once that is done, I'm done.*

It was painful to try to explain something like that to someone I worked for and know that if something happened to me, I wouldn't be able to do the work, but he still didn't care. Working for him depended on my health. If I wasn't healthy, I wouldn't be able to do the work. He'd told me to call him Father, he was supposed to be caring, but he didn't care.

We lived with animals, with wild animals. That was how we got our meat. I would hunt with the gun Mr. Appau bought for me, but it rained so much that the gun might not work properly. The majority of the time I would go into the forest and set traps. We hunted the antelopes. I looked at their footprints to see where they were, then I would set traps. Every morning before I started on the farm, I would go check those traps and see if I caught anything: antelope or crocodiles.

One day I caught a big antelope. I was thinking about eating some of that big meat, but Mr. Appau said we had to sell it. *Great*, I was thinking, *this will bring me a lot of money*. I used my time and skills to trap that antelope, but I soon found out that the proceeds would not be *mine*. It was technically *his* because I worked for him. Everything I earned was for him.

"Hey, Father," I said. "Are we going to cook the intestines? We'll cook the liver and everything, right?"

"No," he said. "We're going to sell the whole antelope."

When we sold it, I didn't know where the money went, of course. It wasn't mine. This really got under my skin. I had set the trap in my free time, so I thought I should be able to sell it for side money, but nope, the proceeds were all his. All the money I was earning for him in the village, he was investing in that city house.

Everything I did, went to him. It was the end of 1994, and I was in slavery.

Palm Wine Tapper

I learned the culture of that village. I learned to understand Mr. Appau. The longer I stayed, the more I learned about his farm and how to work for him.

Three months into the year, he said, "Now that you are very good at weeding, and you understand the whole place, I want you to become a palm wine tapper."

Being a palm wine tapper meant that I was going to fell palm trees and put a tube, rather like a pipe through the tree to drain the palm juice. This sap would collect in a large pot. I would then take this liquid to prepare alcohol similar to tequila, but more powerful.

I didn't know how to do it at first.

"You have to learn," my boss told me.

Each day I would fell five palm trees. My palms became so calloused that they were like stones. Tapping on the ax or machete, I could feel nothing. I learned how to grab a snake head with my palm and not feel anything. I would just grab it and throw it out of my way and move on with what I was doing. If I saw a cobra in the grass by my feet, I would cut off its head and then step over it. By then I was conditioned to be numb, like a stone. I had adapted to every physical and emotional trial that was happening on that farm.

Every morning, I would go down to the river camp where I prepared alcohol using basic chemistry. I collected the liquid that had been released from the tree overnight and placed it inside a 55-gallon barrel and covered the barrel. I left the cover on for three or four days so the liquid could begin to ferment. In this camp, I coiled pipes through the river. I set a fire underneath the barrel and began to boil the liquid, and then piped this vapor through the cooling tubes in the river so it could cool off and not melt the plastic gallon containers I poured it into.

I would be in that camp down by the river from 5:00 am until 2:00 am the next day, running multiple batches of alcohol at once. This process of tapping the felled palm nut trees and fermenting the sap into palm wine was making Mr. Appau money. He wanted me to focus my efforts on the thing that would make him the most money.

This alcohol was so strong that it could not be drunk until it was mixed with other liquids.

I would ferment five barrels of palm wine at a time.

The old man would say, "Hey, go to the next village and get some big men who can help you pull the containers to the train."

Then I would go to the nearby village of Wassa and would hire some big men.

The trains would deliver these barrels to the capital city of Accra. Mr. Appau had people who would meet that train and sell the liquor to a wholesaler who would redistribute it to other customers. They would buy by the gallon and then resell it in bottles.

The money was Mr. Appau's, but I would manage the process. This is when I started to realize the unfairness of the situation I was in. Sure, 50,000 cedis had sounded like a lot of money to me when I first arrived from Togo, but now, knowing how much labor I'd put into making the palm wine and selling it, I knew this was not a fair price for the number of hours I was working and the cruelty I endured when I was only allowed to eat once a day. When I was selling the palm wine, I could see that the old man was pulling in over one million cedis every other week.

That was my new job. I was going to be doing that for the next seven months. I would do this work every day, though I would get a break on the weekends. It wasn't much of a break; we would go to church. Mr. Appau was a big Christian in that village. He was one of the elders in the Methodist Church. Church meant nothing to me, I still had no religious beliefs, but I couldn't say "No, I'm not going to go," because he was in charge.

So every Sunday we would go there and worship.

I didn't have any rights. I couldn't go anywhere unless he sent me there. In that village, I was isolated. It was scary to go to another village through the thick forest. You never knew what was going to happen. The church is a faraway place. We went there with our machetes because a snake could come onto the road, or we would have to use the machetes to trim the trees that have fallen across the road.

Walking along there, we would see green mambas that liked to show themselves off to people. We would see them hanging right above our heads. They were beautiful in the sense that they would not bite you, but they were scary. They blended in and out of the leaves.

It was not easy to get up and go see a friend, not that I made any friends there anyway.

It was pretty tense. I couldn't say what was on my mind, just *yes, yes, yes, yes, yes* for the twelve months so I could get my money. I was trapped.

The old man had every right to beat me up, even though he was old, and I could have beaten the heck out of him, I could not do that because he was my boss.

Sometimes the old man would buy me a new shirt to wear.

"This is going to come out of your 50,000," he would say.

He never really took the money from me, but he made way more from me than he compensated me for.

After church, we would walk back home and relax, at least for the rest of Sunday, we wouldn't do much work. We would just be at home and enjoy ourselves. We would sit down and relax.

We lived in the middle of nowhere. Aside from the times, I would go to church, the only person I would see was the old man.

I felt like I was lost. I started wondering, *do I belong to anybody? Does somebody care about me?* I got no letters, nothing. I didn't hear a thing from my brother who gave me to Mr. Appau. Of course, my family didn't know where I was, and I had no way to contact them. I had left my village without saying goodbye, and they were probably thinking I was dead and they were never going to see me again, like my elder brother, the only other person in my family to go to ninth grade. One day he just disappeared, and we never saw him again. We never found out what happened to him. Was that how it was going to end for me?

At night, one thing that really scared me was the soldier ants. I had never seen these before in Togo. They lived in the thick forest and loved the scent of palm nuts, especially when they were boiled.

When we boiled palm nuts and squeezed them, we tossed aside the remaining husk. We didn't put them inside a bin to prevent attracting vermin. These cast-away husks attracted soldier ants who came to eat the palm nut husks. The smell invited them. When they came, while I was sleeping for those few hours at night, I would be in my bed and feel them biting me.

I learned that when soldier ants bit me, they didn't release. They would bite me and hold on. If I tried to knock one-off, the body might fall off, but the head would still be inside me, biting me. I had to take my fingers and pull out the head. They didn't go one by one. They went as a group of millions.

I would jump up, and they were all over the house. Nobody could sleep that night. Nobody. When the soldier ants turned up, we had to burn some stuff, like kerosene or wood fire to drive them away, so we could go back to sleep. If we didn't do that, we were going to be standing there for the rest of the night. Those ants turned up very frequently. For the twelve months I lived there, they came practically every other day.

The only good thing about the soldier ants was that they drove away the snakes. I would be sitting in the house and see the snakes up in the roof stretch and move away fast. That's when I would know the soldier ants were coming.

It was crazy how scary it was living like this with snakes and soldier ants in the house, but once I'd been doing it long enough, I got used to it.

Counting the Days

Once I got into the middle of the 12 months, I started counting down the months. I was counting down the days. I could not *wait* to gain my freedom. I was learning a lot, but given the way I was learning it, those were the worst months of my life.

When I was working there, a flying spider bit me on the back of my neck. It was even more painful than the time in Togo when I was bitten by a snake as this spider was very poisonous. While I was cutting my way, weeding underneath the palm trees, it flew over and bit me.

"Ouch!" I cried.

My neck became stiff, and I couldn't turn my neck normally. I had to call the old man. One good thing about him was he had medical supplies in his house. He put some antibiotic cream on it. It took me three days to be able to get up. The old man spent a lot of time taking care of me and then he used that against me as if I called the spider to come and bite me. For three days I didn't go to work, and he did all the cooking.

After that, he said, "Three days you didn't do this. Three days you didn't do that. Now you're going to have to work from 5:00 am to 6:00 pm. Don't come home in between. If you're hungry, maybe you can eat pineapples or bananas."

There was fruit everywhere, but given all the labor I was doing, fruit could only sustain me so much. I weighed one hundred and eighteen pounds then and was very skinny. Very, very skinny with no excess body fat.

He used that spider bite against me quite often.

After six or eight months, he realized I was going to leave, and he wanted to keep me, so he started treating me better and with some respect.

Once we sat down and had a conversation about what I wanted to do.

"Do you want to work for me again?" he asked. "Another year?"

Oh, Lord, no, I was thinking, but I didn't say anything right away.

"What do you think of me? My family?"

Why now? I thought. *Why now do you want me to assess you? You could have been nice from the beginning and then maybe I would want to stay.*

"Do you want to be here? Do you think I'm treating you badly or do you think I'm treating you nicely?"

Suddenly, he wanted to know.

"No, no," I said. "You didn't treat me badly. Everything was fine. You treated me like your child. I enjoyed it."

I said these things because I wanted to get out of there.

"Look, son," Mr. Appau said one day. "You only have about four months left in your contract. You're still *mine*. From now on, there will be no more playing around. I want you to work from Monday to Sunday. There will be no more going to church."

I could see then that I only had four months, and he wanted to use those four months to make as much money off me as he can. After all that I've done already, earning him so much money weeding, collecting his pineapples, fermenting the palm wine, and trapping the antelopes, it was still not enough for him.

When he said I should work from Monday to Sunday, I think that was when my curiosity over what my father told me before he died kicked in. That is when everything started sinking in again about what he said about generosity and a person's actions coming back to him. Maybe they wouldn't come back right away, but they would come to that person's children or grandchildren.

Here I am, I thought. *Working for this man who does not appreciate who I am. Who does not appreciate what I've done for him?*

By then, I could speak Twi with him. I was very good with Twi. I could also speak English very well with him.

I couldn't stop thinking. *This person thinks I'm not enough or that what I've done is not enough. He wants me to spend all week Monday through Sunday working. I have to think about myself. What does he think I am? Am I not a human being? Am I not one of his children? Does he see me as something else?*

Whenever his wife came to that village it would be one week of hell. She was worse than the old man, actually. She would be yelling at me the whole week.

"You don't even know how much money we're going to pay you! That's a lot of money we're going to pay you! So you got to do everything we want you to do. And you have to do it quickly and finish it quickly, and do something else quickly."

Whenever she would come, it would feel like the end of my life.

I didn't have any freedom.

The old man would not say anything to her. It seemed like the wife was in control of everything.

She would say, "Hey, you gotta wash this stuff for me. You gotta wash my stuff. You gotta do this. You gotta do that."

If someone was observing me, they'd see me running around, back and forth, trying to keep up with it all. If I sat down for a second, I was always ready to hop back up because I knew she would be calling me to get up and do something for her.

She would ask me to cook food. I would pound the food with a full-size mortar and pestle until my hands were calloused. When the food was all prepared, she would not let me eat any.

"Hey, can you give some to Yaw?" the old man asked.

"No," she would say.

I would sit down, and she would say, "Oh, I forgot. Can you go pound the palm nut? Because we boiled it, and I need you to pound it so the oil can come out."

I would be pounding all by myself until maybe twelve or one am and I had to get up at five or five-thirty to work on the farm. If I wasn't lucky, and the soldier ants came in that night, that night was going to be the worst night.

I would do all that she asked. She was the worst person I ever met.

"Go do this," she'd say. She would see me doing it, and she'd say, "You haven't finished?" Then she would tell me to do something else.

Hello, I'd be thinking. *How do you expect me to divide myself? You didn't buy me, remember? Am I a slave here? I'm working and I'm getting 50,000, but this is too much to ask.*

"I'm paying you," she'd say. "And before I pay you, that's what you have to do."

I shrugged my shoulders and got the work done.

When she came, she would stay for one week. That one week would be hell. I would pray to God, *let her go, let the week end so quickly so that she can go the boss and I will be free.*

Whenever she came, that's what would be happening. When she spoke to me like that I thought, *Now I speak Twi, I speak a little bit of English, and I'm good at French. I've got three months left. I have to strategize. I have to think. Do I want to stay here?*

I had the option to renew my contract with Mr. Appau for another year if I wanted to. But I said no, I am not going to renew. I am going to *try* something else because I was educated. Even though I didn't finish eighth grade doesn't mean I'm not educated. I just don't want to stay on the farm anymore. I want to do something else. That is the kind of vision that I had. I want to do something else. Farming and working for someone else were not enough for me.

I would get the 50,000 cedis in three months' time, but would it be enough for me to actually do what I wanted to do?

These were my thoughts when he told me I should work from Monday to Sunday. I thought about it. *I've survived nine months. I can survive another three months. I can survive it.*

With three months left to go, my brother, the one who gave me to Mr. Appau, came to visit. In all those nine months he never showed up, he never called, he never sent any communication through my boss. He didn't even ask, "Hey, how are you doing?" He could have taken my picture and sent it to my mother, to let her know I was still alive, but he did none of that.

"Tell me," he said, that day he came to visit. "What are your experiences working with this nice man?" He gestured to Mr. Appau who was listening to the conversation. We were all down in the river camp where I made palm wine.

I sat down for ten minutes and didn't say a word to him. I was upset, very, very upset. Angry. Regretting the time I saw him at home when he was so well dressed. Now I was sitting here in the swamp. I didn't even own a nice shirt. I hadn't been to any markets. I didn't go anywhere, not even to church anymore. And he was sitting down here asking me what my experience is. I was so angry I felt like I was going to get up and slap him. But I remembered my father saying, "there is nothing good that comes your way that is not hard to find. It takes a lot of courage. Any good thing is hard to come by. You may be mistreated, but it is up to you how you receive it, or you accept it, and how you brush it off and move on. That is the only way you can survive."

When my father's words came into my mind, I stood up and said, "Brother, it was good. I enjoyed everything. The old man is a very nice person."

Mr. Appau was standing right there, so I was sure to praise him.

"I wish I could renew my contract with him. I really like him so much. I like his wife. His wife is really, really a nice person."

I said all of this sarcastically. Mr. Appau knew I didn't like his wife. But me saying that in front of him and in front of my brother, he realized I was saying it sarcastically because there was no way I was going to renew my contract with him. No way.

"So," my brother said. "Do you want to sign up for another year?"

"I wish I could," I said. "But I just can't. I want to try something different."

"Okay." He nodded his head. "Now, this time they're going to offer 30,000 more for another year. You will get 80,000 instead of 50,000."

"Brother," I said. "Thank you, but I want to try something else. This has been a great experience. I've learned a lot being in this village, but now it is time for me to move on to something else."

"So what are you going to do?" he asked.

"I don't know," I said. "But I want to go back to Kumasi with you and figure out something."

"Okay, when your three months are finished, he will bring you to me with your money. When you take it, if you want to go back home, and see your family, then you can come back."

I went back to making palm wine, and the two of them kept talking.

It was harder for them to manipulate me then because I understood Twi. I could speak English. They could no longer say anything I wasn't aware of. I realized that my brother was suggesting something to the old man to convince me to do one more year. The old man had a cacao farm, and someone else was looking after it. My brother wanted to take care of it. In order to get it, he needed to convince me to do another year so maybe my salary would have been 80,000 and he would get that man's cacao farm to take care of it. So that was the trade off for him.

When I said no, the only way he didn't lose that cacao farm was he told the old man he'd go off and get him another guy from Togo to replace me.

After I realized that I was nothing but a bargaining chip to my brother, for his own cut of the money, I started thinking about what those 50,000 cedis would do for me. With the money, I would have to buy a bus ticket. I didn't have shoes. I didn't have nice pants. I didn't have nice stuff. I didn't have the cologne my brother wore when he came to my village and enticed me on this trip. I didn't have any of these things. If I tried to buy them with 50,000, how much would be left for me to take back to my mother?

Okay, I decided. *I'm not going to go home right away. First, I need to make more money.*

"This is Your Wife"

When the three months were up, my boss said, "Okay, now you've done a good job. You have been a very good kid to me. I've received many kids here, but they've never been like you. I want to say 'thank you so much.' I want to give you an extra 30,000 cedis for being a good boy to me."

Instead of giving me 50,000 cedis, he was going to give me 80,000.

"Thank you so much, sir," I said, thinking of all the times I wanted to quit, to run out of that village and break my contract. But I hadn't quit. I had survived and I was going to get my money. "You have been great to me. I mean, we worked together. We ate together and all that. Even though sometimes I felt like you were too harsh on me, I understand that part because I was working for money. I understood that part and I want to thank you for teaching me a lot. Now if I go somewhere else, I can do things by myself. I can prepare alcohol. Thank you so much. I've learned a lot."

Now it was 1995, and I was done being a slave to this man. But that wasn't the end of my time in Ghana. I had to go back to my brother's place.

My brother was living on the old man's cacao farm one hour and thirty minutes by bus from Kumasi. The old man took me there.

That day my brother gathered together with other village people from Togo, and they were awaiting my arrival. I knew I was expected to buy alcohol for them to drink to say thank you.

I was thinking, *you guys took me to this man, and I hustled for twelve months and now I'm coming back, and you guys want me to buy the drinks and thank you guys for giving me the opportunity to work with this man*. It felt unbelievable. But I did it. That was the tradition, the custom for them.

"Go and order," they said. "We'll give you the money, and then you'll pay."

I bought the drinks. We all sat down, and we drank. Now Mr. Appau had to dig into his pocket and bring the money out. He counted it all, then gave it to another man to count to make sure the amount was correct. Three people counted that money before they gave it to me.

After they gave me the 50,000, my boss stood up and said, "This child here has been a very good boy to me. He respected my rules. Even though I did some stuff he could have disrespected me, he never disrespected me. For that reason, I'm giving him another 30,000. That will be 80,000 in total."

When they heard that, they were like, "Okay, that 30,000 cedis, you can give it to us and we will buy food."

"No," I said. "That 30,000 is *mine*. And mine only. I'm not giving it to you guys."

I watched them fold their arms across their chests. "Oh, okay," they said. "Now you understand the system better than us. Now you don't want to give us anything."

I started noticing their jealousy. There was plenty to eat on that farm, the only food we might need to buy would be meat, and we would only need a few cedis for that. The extra 30,000 was *mine*.

I had to think fast, like the day I was trapped in the palm nut tree with that viper.

My brother had a wife. We were all from the same village. But my brother was a drunkard. He would drink and drink and drink and drink and go crazy.

"I'm going to stay with you for two weeks," I told my brother. "And I'll help you weed your farm."

I knew that while I was weeding, I could be thinking and planning what to do next.

"Okay," he said. "Stay with me for two weeks. Then we can find something else for you to do."

"Okay," I agreed.

Those two weeks were hell. It was even worse than when I was with my boss and his wife would come to visit.

My brother drank so much. When we finished working, I would stay home, and he would go out to the small village bar. Whenever he got drunk, he would come home and beat his wife like crazy. I would try to separate them, and he would hit me. I knew I could beat him, but I wanted to show him respect. I didn't want to beat him in front of his wife. But the way he was treating her was ridiculous. It was not how any human being would like to be treated.

After they were separated, they would be sitting together. They would team up and start insulting me.

When he was off drinking, I would try to tell her things. "Look this has been going on for…I don't know…I never lived here with you. But for the past week, I've seen all these things. I don't see how anyone could enjoy this. I'm trying to help. Instead of you being by my side so we can stop him from abusing you, you will run under the cacao trees in the middle of the night, and he'll be chasing you. Is that what you want? After that, you go back to him as if nothing happened. Then you guys team up and start insulting me."

I couldn't understand why she couldn't hear me. I was trying to *help* her. Did she like being beaten? Maybe she didn't know where to go. Maybe she didn't have anywhere to go and she accepted the situation as something she had to put up with. I don't know. The next day, they would be going around laughing as if nothing had happened. She didn't say, "I can't take this anymore." Maybe she understood that her husband was a drunkard and that's why he was beating her and she just accepted it.

I would keep stepping in between them to separate them, and he would hit me.

Finally, I said, "Brother. If you hit me again, I'm going to hit you back. Don't hit me."

"You're sleeping with my wife!" he shouted at me.

Boy, I thought, shaking my head in disbelief at his allegation.

My brother called the forest police. In Ghana, the forest is protected by officers wearing uniforms, but technically they're not police. These guys would come around and make sure people didn't cut certain trees down in the village.

My brother confided in the forest police that *I* was sleeping with his wife, and he wanted to kill me.

The forest police came to the house. When I spoke to the officer, he seemed very educated.

"Sir," I said. "This is what is happening. I'm going to tell you my story."

After telling him my story, the officer said, "Whoa. Yeah, you're right. But you know what we're going to do. We're not going to make him look stupid. I understand. I know he's a drunkard. He gets drunk and goes crazy, but this is what we're going to do. We're going to tell him he is right, and then we're going to go. Later on, we'll figure out what to do."

That wasn't the end. The next night my brother did the same thing. He came up, he was drunk. He beat his wife. I separated them again.

I said, "This time if you hit me, I am going to slap you."

"I know you're sleeping with my wife," he said.

I couldn't understand how he could think this. She was older than me, so there was no way I would be sleeping with her.

I said, "You don't even know how that old man treated me. You never went there to see me. And you never asked him to bring me back so you could see me. And now you're sitting down here telling me that I'm sleeping with your wife? No way. I cannot take it."

After only one week, I was forced to leave the house because it was too much for me.

This was May 1995. My brother said, "You know what, if you don't leave my house, I am going to kill you, because every time I am out, you are sleeping with my wife."

I replied, "You know what, brother? I am not in any position to sleep with your wife. She is even older than me. I don't have that intention. If you want me to leave, I will leave."

All the farms in that area were cacao farms, and I met someone who was a cacao farmer.

He said to me, "Hey, maybe you can come and look after this cacao farm. You'll make the harvest, then let me know how many bags you get. We will share the profit. You will take one-third, and I will take two-thirds."

"Okay," I said. "If that's the case, I'm going to do it. I will go with this cacao farmer."

The next day I went and looked at the cacao farm. It was very nice. It wasn't that big, but for me, a single person, it was fine. For running a larger cacao farm, I would need to have a wife to work with and take the harvest. The man plucked the cacao nuts, while the wife gathered them. But, I would be the only one there, so I would pluck, then gather them up myself.

I left my brother's place and went to look after the cacao farm.

Now that I was away from my brother's drinking and fighting, I could finally relax. I was so relieved to be in my own place, with no one bossing me around. I could finally start to recover from the horrible time at Mr. Appau's farm. I praised God that it was over and I was able to get out. The only thing that kept me moving through those twelve months was my vision.

When it was time to harvest the cacao nuts, I plucked nine bags. The owner took six bags, and I took three bags. In November of 1995, I sold the three bags for 400,000 cedis. This was huge money.

Now it was time for me to strategize. There was nothing in my life that had ever been enough for me. I mean this in a very positive way. Instead of seeing myself in the present, I always envisioned myself in the future. I think that is what was driving me. Not so many people see it that way. But I always see myself in the future.

I thought, *should I go back to Togo? Or should I stay in Ghana?*

I had been away from home for over a year and hadn't communicated with my family in any way. *Should I go there and say hello to* them? *Or should I just keep on going? No*, I thought. *I'm going to go. At least visit my mother and then come back to Ghana and see what I can do.*

I could see more opportunities for myself in Ghana than in Togo. I had a vision of teaching and going somewhere else. Ghana was the only place I could catch up with my life.

I had a friend in that village, a very good friend. He wasn't a Togolese, but Ghanaian. I was interested in his sister, so I started hanging out with him. After work, he'd come down to the farm, and then his sister would come along and cook some food, and we would eat together.

One day I started telling him my thoughts about what I should try to do now that I'd finished my work on the cacao farm.

He said, "I can see you're picking up English very well, so why don't you try to teach French in one of those private schools?"

"Do you think they will take me?"

"Yeah, because you speak French. And you speak English. So it's easy."

"Well, maybe I will try."

That is how my strategy came together.

I learned that discussing your vision with people who have the same interests will help you achieve that goal. People who don't have those same interests will try to squash your ideas.

But this man made a good suggestion, and this was when I started thinking about how to go teach French.

I bought some shoes for 500 cedis and some nice clothes for another 100 cedis. For another 500 cedis, I bought a fancy multicolored shirt that some people might think is over the top, but I don't care what they say. My outfit wasn't 100% matching, but at least I had some nice things to wear, so who cared? They were *my* clothes. I was seventeen years old, and for the first time in my life, I had my own nice things to wear. I bought some stuff for my mother, clothes for my sisters, I bought things for my half-brothers.

So I went home, and everyone was excited to see me. They were completely surprised to see me, and as I'd expected, I found out they *had* been thinking I was dead, like my elder brother who we never saw again. He had dropped out of ninth grade and left to travel. Nobody ever heard from him again.

When I think of my own dangers, crossing wild rivers, facing the Dagomba tribe in Northern Ghana, nearly being bitten by a viper, etc., etc., etc., it is easy to think how he could have dropped off the earth.

But I liked to think he had survived somehow.

The very first day my mother saw me, she was so excited. She was like, "*Wow*! My son is now a *man*!"

"Yep," I said. "I'm a man, Mommy."

The second or third day I was home, I saw a woman I hadn't seen before in the house.

My mother set a plate of food in front of me and said, "Son, the food you are about to eat, you know who cooked it for you? The woman you just saw," my mother said, pointing back into the house. "*She* cooked it for you. She's a very good cook."

In my village, "very good cook" is code for "wife material." Now I could see that they wanted to give me a wife. My mother wanted to marry me off.

My mother went on. "She's a very good cook. I know where she's from. I know the family. They're a very respected family. She's here to be your wife."

I cocked my head sideways. "What? To be my wife? I don't know her. I haven't spoken to any of her family members. I don't know who she *is*. How am I just going to be somebody's husband? We never had any conversation."

I wasn't just going to marry someone I didn't know.

Besides, as I told my mother, "Mom, I think I have a vision ahead of me. If I marry her, right now, I'm not going to accomplish that vision."

"Son, look," my mother said. "Look at your mates." She waved her hand around the village. "Those guys that you were going to school with? They're *married*. They have *kids*. Some of them already have two wives. This guy here has two wives. This one there has three wives. They have kids all over. You know, you're supposed to get married and build your own family."

I could see myself again as that young boy, herding cattle on the mountain and watching my age mates coming home from school, learning those songs I didn't yet know. I could see this was just like that time. I had other things I was supposed to be doing now than what my age mates were doing.

I had a very, very negative view about wives. I wasn't even dating. I had a very negative view of women and marriage. I thought I was not even going to get married. The way my brother and his wife were fighting all the time and the way the old man's wife treated me had soured my view of wives. I was not ready for this. I had my vision lined up.

This place was not enough for me. I wanted to get somewhere else.

"Mom," I said. "It's okay. Let them get married. My life is coming. I have to go back to Ghana because I have to do something that none of them have done."

"What are you going to do?" she asked.

"I'm going back to teach French."

My mom looked up at me. "Wow. Really?"

"Yep."

The next thing I knew, the woman they'd found for me to marry was crying and saying, "Well, you know, they trained me to be here. I wanted to be your wife. And your mother told me a lot about *you*. You can't just leave me here. You have—"

"Look," I said. "Thank you for the food. You're a really good cook. You cook really nice, but I just don't have time for marriage right now."

She was still crying. "Do you want to grow old before you get married?"

"Uh-uh. I'm not going to grow old before I get married, but it's not time for me to get married right now."

"So what are you going to do?" she asked.

"I don't know," I told her.

But I knew I would figure it out.

3

A New Adventure in Kumasi

After one week at home, I left for Ghana without telling my family. Once again, I didn't tell my mom goodbye. I didn't tell my brothers goodbye or that I was going back to Ghana.

If I told them that I was going back, they would say, "You have to go with your wife." I didn't want that to happen. I wanted to go back and *then* tell them where I was and what I was trying to do.

In January (going to February) of 1996, I returned to Kumasi, the first big city where I'd ever been.

Fighting Over Benches

I told my brother, the drunkard, who lived on the cacao farm outside Kumasi, "Hey, I came back. But I'm not coming to you. I am in Kumasi now."

In the city, I didn't know anybody. I arrived with my bags. Besides not wanting to see my brother, I also didn't want to go to old Mr. Appau's house. I wanted to start a completely new adventure.

After I got off the bus, I sat on a bench where people were selling food by the roadside. I sat down to eat. There was an old man who came and sat beside me. He was very old, so I bought my food and some for him. We began to eat.

While we were eating, he said, "Wow, nobody ever bought food for me. At least not like this."

I shrugged my shoulders. "You're an old man. It's okay for me to buy food for you."

"No," he said. "I have money to buy the food myself."

"But it's okay," I said. "Let me buy it for you."

"Where are you from?" he asked. "Because Ashanti people are not so generous like this," he said, referring to his own tribe. "Where are you from?"

That's when I started telling him my story of where I came from.

"Okay," he said. "That explains why you are so generous. Where you're from, people are very generous."

"I've come to Kumasi to teach," I said. "But I don't know the schools yet and I don't have anywhere to stay."

His face puzzled up. "How are you coming to the city to teach without knowing *anybody* or without even knowing the school where you're coming to teach?"

I shrugged my shoulders. "I don't know. I just thought I was ready to teach."

"You know what?" he said. "I can help you. I don't have a room, but I have a hallway at the main entrance of my house. There is a bench on either side. If you can sleep on this bench until you get your own apartment, great."

"Sir," I said, snapping my fingers over my shoulder. "I'm going to take it. Because I don't know *anybody*."

After we finished eating, I walked back to his house with him and he showed me the benches. "Okay!" I said. I laughed that someone who was coming to teach French would have to sleep on a bench. But I didn't want to rent a house or an apartment because I didn't have the money.

"If this is where you're going to sleep," the man said. "Take it now."

As I lay down on this bench and tried to sleep, I thought of my father saying, "If you are generous, people will be generous to you." When I sat down with the old man, I wasn't thinking of getting a favor from him. It wasn't anything calculated, I just bought him food because he was an old man, the way I would have bought food for my father. In my village, this is what I would have done. I just decided to buy the food for him and that action that he took in offering me the bench, reminded me of my father.

I slept on the benches for free, but I had to help the man and his family buy food for the house. I got up early every morning and fetched water for them. I pounded their food with a full-size mortar and pestle to thank them for being generous enough to give me that place to sleep.

It was a compound house, and many people with children were renting rooms. I quickly understood why the old man had urged me to grab the bench early.

Whether it was raining or not, people liked to sit down there on those benches. There was shade and protection from the rain, and people liked to gather there to talk. My problem with that was this: Boys and girls my age didn't like sleeping in their father's room, they wanted to sleep on the benches. Sometimes it was hot inside, and cooler on those benches. We would fight over those benches. Whoever gets there first gets to sleep there. That was it. Nobody else could take it away from him.

We would be looking strategically at what time we thought we could get in there and sit on those benches and never get up, even if something was biting me or I had to go use the restroom, I didn't want to get up, because I knew the moment I got up, somebody else was going to come to sit on it, and once they sat on it, they'd sleep on it, and then I wouldn't have anywhere to sleep. If there was no place to sleep, I would sit on the cement floor and put my body against the wall. It wasn't only me because there were so many children in that compound, and we only had two benches. The houses were not big enough to contain five children in each bedroom. When it was raining, we couldn't sit. We had to stand until whenever it stopped and then sleep on that wet floor.

Two Unripe Mangoes

One day I was walking and saw a teacher walking too. I could tell he was a teacher because he had a certain bag that teachers carry and nice shoes. Teachers walk a lot, and I could see the sides of his shoes were worn out. He also had about three pens (red, blue, and black)

I approached him, "Hey! Where are you teaching?"

"This school, down there."

"I want to teach French. But I don't know what to do."

"Oh!" he said. "There are international schools where you can teach. You just have to write a letter of application or letter of employment, and they will employ you."

Even though I could speak a little English, I couldn't write in it. I told this teacher, "I can write in French. But do you have someone who can write it in English for me?"

He helped me find somebody who would help.

"I can write you a letter of employment," he said.

"I can write it in French and then you could translate it," I said.

"No, that's too long. I'm just going to write for you."

"Okay, thank you."

The man wrote a paragraph about me and why I wanted to teach.

I took the letter to a school known as Pax International School. This was March 1996.

I went to the school, and the proprietor said, "Do you want to teach?"

"Yep," I nodded my head.

"What do you know?"

"I can teach French."

"Okay," she said. "We will take you. We'll pay you 15,000 cedis a month."

"Yeah, it's okay," I said. "I will take it."

All the money that I had from my previous jobs is gone. I had been generous to that old man and given food money to his house.

I kept my money in my bag. Because I slept in the hallway, I was afraid that the old man's kids, young boys, and girls might go in my bag and take some stuff. The old man assured me they wouldn't and let me keep my bag in his room. At night, I would sleep in the hallway. In the morning, I had to wake up and get dressed and go teach, and sometimes, the door was locked from the inside. I had to wait for them to get up. I couldn't go there and knock. Once they opened the door, I would take buckets to fetch water, and come back, take a shower, and go to school.

I had no money coming in, only money going out. When I looked, all of my money was gone. I was left with nothing, but thank God I got the teaching job, hoping every month I would get something.

A NEW ADVENTURE IN KUMASI

That month that I started teaching, I decided to move out of the old man's house. Because it was a compound house with different rooms and people renting. The old man had five boys living in his room. He owned the whole house. They cooked food at night, but I decided I had to leave. Sleeping on a bench was too much for me. I was tired of having to fight for it.

I decided to go to the school compound and sleep there. I figured I could wake up early, and people wouldn't know that I slept there.

I talked to the security guard who was guarding the compound. "Hey, I want to come and sleep here at night and wake up early."

"Oh yeah," he said. "You can do that."

I had a place to sleep, but I didn't have food. I didn't know what to do. I really didn't know any of the other teachers yet, so I asked them for something. My pride was stopping me from telling them that I didn't have any money. I still needed to study them to see if it was a good idea to ask.

So I went to the proprietor of the school and said, "Please, can you give me at least 5,000 in advance pay? When the month ends, you would only pay me 10,000."

She looked at me and said, "You haven't even finished one week yet. And you want an advance salary? No. I'm not going to give it to you."

I felt like someone was sticking a needle into the middle of my heart. I had to sit down to think.

Whoa! I don't know anybody. I have no family. Nobody. I can't ask anyone for 1,000 or 2,000 cedis to buy food. So what am I supposed to do?

"Really?" I asked. "I need some money to buy food so I can *teach*."

"Nope," she said again.

When she said that, a surge hit me. I was already hungry. That statement from her just kicked me. If this woman could not advance me some money, I would be out of luck because I don't have anyone, I can ask for a loan.

Whoa. So what am I supposed to do?

I looked at her face and saw she wasn't even looking at me.

Someone had told me that in city life people don't care about each other, the way they do in the village.

So this is city life, I thought.

Even though she knew that I didn't have money to buy food, she just thought, *I don't care about you.*

Okay, I thought. *It's fine.* But then, before I walked out, I said, "Can you do some*thing*? Just a little bit."

"Hey," she said. "If you want to teach, go teach. If you don't want to teach, you can pack your bags and leave."

I put both hands up in the stop position. "I want to teach. I want to teach."

I walked out of there hungry and hurt.

I went to the classroom and waited for the canteen to come, but it didn't come. The school had a canteen that provided food for students, and teachers could sometimes get something to eat. It wasn't all the time. It depended, some days they gave it to the teachers. Students paid for it and got it every day. Teachers didn't pay for it so, according to the lady who served it, she was doing us a favor.

Sometimes, I would wait until the morning when the food would be served, and I would eat.

But now I had a class I had to teach. I thought *this is too much for me.* But I didn't have any choice.

Standing up in front of the students and teaching them on an empty stomach was hard. They would make noise, but I wouldn't have the energy to tell them to sit down. Other students were jumping on me, and I didn't have the strength to engage with them. That was a challenging moment.

After class, I waited again for the canteen to come, and when it came, I ate. It was *something* but wasn't particularly nutritious. It was peanut butter soup and rice. That's it. The soup had no meat. They put Maggi, a seasoning sauce, in it to make it sweet. If there was no meat, the Maggi made the soup more palatable. The soup was really watery so they could feed all the kids. One bowl of rice and that soup and you were supposed to be good for the day.

This is the city, I thought again.

Even though I was hungry, I didn't want to go back to that compound house where I had been sleeping on the benches. Once I move on, I don't look back. That is my motto. When I end a relationship with someone, it's over. I just move forward. The reason why things didn't work, the same thing is going to be there, and it won't help me move forward.

If I was in the village I could just go into the forest and cut things to eat. I thought of going back to my brother's cocoa farm, which was an hour and thirty-minute bus ride, but then I thought of my vision. Ever since I was born, I've had a vision. I said to myself, *remember where you've come from.* I remembered myself as a young boy, wanting to go to school, running out of the house naked. *I was born with that vision.* I've always wanted to get to *somewhere* bigger than myself. When I thought of going back, the vision came up and said, *remember where you're going. If you go back to the village, you're not going to get to where you want to be.*

So can you hold on and learn how the whole system works? Because you see people living and walking around the city. If they are here, then I can also be here.

There's no reason for me to go back to that village, I thought. This was how I gained strength. Even though I was hungry as hell, I got strength because I had a vision. Staying at that school and teaching and seeing where my life would go was very important to me.

There was one specific day that I could not *hold*. I was *dying*. I was *dying of hunger*. That fateful day was a Tuesday, a day when there was no canteen for the teachers. I slept Monday night, but Tuesday night I was so hungry I could not sleep. I was in trouble. I had to make it through to Wednesday to get to the canteen.

I hadn't eaten in so long that I could not even drink water. There was nothing in my stomach. I sat in the school and wondered what to do. I would sleep on the school benches, then wake up early and take a shower, so the students didn't know I was sleeping in the school. I laid down on the bench, but I could not sleep. My stomach would not let me sleep. I got up and walked around and tried to do something to make myself sleep, but still, I could not sleep.

Luckily for me, there was a mango tree in the school compound. On the top of that mango tree, I saw two very small, very green mangoes.

I told myself, *you know if I can get one of these, bite it, at least it could help me drink water and sleep.*

It was midnight. I climbed that mango tree, plucked one of those mangoes, and bit into it. Thank God I was able to reach where the mangoes were. Otherwise, I didn't have the strength to get down. My legs were shaking. As soon as I grabbed it, I bit it again and again and again. It was so far from being ripe that it was not a good thing to do. I bit it, closed my eyes, chewed it, and swallowed it. I ate the whole mango, including the seeds. Then I felt stabilized. I was eating it while I was coming down. The way my legs had been shaking I probably would have fallen if I'd tried to climb down without eating it first.

After eating that mango, I could drink water, sleep, and wait until the morning when I could get a canteen meal and eat. Then I would be able to teach again that day.

Teaching French at Cambridge International School

After teaching at Pax International School at Asuoyeboah for two months, I said to myself, *you know what? Do what you always do best. Strategize. Think.*

After two months I went to the proprietor and said, "Look, this salary does not help me. Fifteen thousand cedis a month is not helping me."

She shrugged her shoulders.

I could see I wasn't going to get anywhere with her, so I started asking other teachers, "Hey, do you guys know any other school where I can go and teach?

They said, "There are so many international schools here. You can go to one and teach."

I learned that discussing my vision with people who have the same interests as me will help me achieve that goal. But I already knew that people who didn't have those same interests would try to squash them.

I was always strategic, always thinking about what to do next.

I found the biggest international school in Kumasi: Cambridge International School. If I could get the opportunity to teach there, I would be set for life. Those kids' parents are from the US, France, and Germany, so I figured they must pay their teachers a good wage. I went there and dropped off my application.

The proprietor saw me, and said, "You're too young to teach here in this school."

"Sir," I said. "I'm not too young. I can do the job. I can teach."

"Whoa," he said. "Really?"

"Yep." I nodded my head. *What was he thinking, too young? I was nineteen years old.*

"Okay. We're going to give you a test."

The tests never finish, I thought to myself. *They keep giving me tests, just to make sure I can do* it.

If I passed the test, they would employ me to teach there. Because it was a big school, they were going to be careful with whom they hired. They wanted only the best teachers for their students.

The test was that the proprietor and some other administration members would take me to ninth grade so I could teach those kids, and the administrators would be sitting there observing me and watching the reaction of the students. If the students reacted positively, they would take me. If they reacted negatively, then that would be it, they weren't going to hire me.

They walked me to JSS3, Junior Secondary School. They gave me chalk, and the board was there. "Okay," they said. "The floor is yours. Teach them."

I hadn't been to ninth grade myself, and here I was standing in front of ninth-grade students I was supposed to teach. I was nineteen, and these kids were fourteen, but I knew I could do it.

Teaching French in an anglophone country is different from teaching it in a francophone country. The levels are different for non-native speakers. We weren't striving for fluency. My job was to give these ninth graders a basic understanding of French.

In that class, JSS3, there were ninety-five students. Some of the students were taller than me, and many were bigger than me. These were physically mature kids who had benefited from good nutrition all their lives.

I took the chalk. The owner of the school was sitting to my left. The class teacher was sitting in front. The assistant director was on my right. They were all sitting there waiting for me to start.

I started teaching. Even though my English was not really good enough for the students to understand me, I was using only French. I told them that if you want to teach somebody to understand and use a language, you teach in that language. Even if the students didn't understand all my words, they understood my actions. I was using all my gestures. The kids were very interactive.

"Come here," I said in French and waved towards me. They came.

"Go," I said and pushed away with my hands. They went.

At the end of the forty-five-minute lesson, the students were jumping up and down saying, "Yes, yes. We want this. We want that." They were giving me the double thumbs up.

The students didn't know I was being interviewed for the job as their teacher. But they clearly liked my style of teaching.

I learned later that they'd had many French teachers come and go. These teachers were all Ghanaian-trained French teachers who didn't get the correct pronunciation or give the feel of someone teaching the whole lesson in French.

The proprietor took me back to his office and asked me, "What did you do to them?"

"What do you mean?" I asked.

"They were happy," he said. "They accepted you. And it felt like they understood everything that you said. Even if they did not understand, their reaction was like they were happy to work with someone like you."

"I don't know, sir," I said. "If that's their reaction, then take me."

They gave me the job. Finally, I got a well-paid teaching job. They offered me 45,000 cedis a month. There were 5,000 students at this school. It was part of the biggest private schools in Kumasi, and possibly, in Ghana, and one of the best-dressed students and teachers in Kumasi.

One funny thing that happened when I started teaching at Cambridge International was that I met the teacher I'd seen in the street, the one who helped me write my letter of employment for my first teaching job. His name is Mr. Manu Frimpong, a Twi language teacher.

I got my own apartment half a mile from the school. In Ghana, a house is rented by the year, sometimes two or three years of rent are needed all at once. I borrowed some money from a good colleague of mine.

"Once I start teaching, I will give you another year, and we'll go from there,"

I told the landlady.

"Okay," she said.

I began teaching French. My English still wasn't very good at this time. I wrote it in French and translated it into English. I asked them to read English, and I listened to how they read it. I learned English from them as they learned French from me.

I formed a French club. Students started speaking French with me, and we had conversations. We had end-of-term activities, and I would invite the parents in to hear their children speak French. They would make short recitations and put on short plays. We would be telling stories in French, while another student would be translating them into English so the parents could understand.

"Wow. This is great." The parents would rave about these recitations.

I no longer had to buy my own shoes because my parents would be sending me shoes.

One kid came in and said, "Hey. My father said 'take these shoes.'"

It made me think back to when I started school in Togo, and one of my poor teachers would shine his shoes every night, only to become dusty again by the next day. Now I was that teacher, but I was far beyond the teacher from my primary school.

Not only did I get my salary, the shoes, and other gifts, but I was also making money as a tutor. I would go to the students' homes, grouping five students in one house, and help them with their repetitions. Each student paid 95000 to 100000 cedis, enough to pay one year's rent. I was making half a million cedis per month doing that.

Now I can cook for myself. I could have a TV. in my bedroom.

My brothers would come to my house, and I would give them money to take back home to the village.

In 2000, I heard a rumor that my eldest brother, the one who had left the village in the ninth grade, the one we thought must be dead, had settled in the Ivory Coast, and I went on a trip to look for him. While I was there, I found him and confirmed that he was alive. He had opened up a shop and changed his identity from a Togolese to Ivorian and had an Ivorian last name. He even had an Ivorian wife. I started to notice from the way he was speaking about government and politics that he had been radicalized. His identity was so completely Ivorian that he was not going to make it out.

Not long after my visit, civil war broke out in the Ivory Coast. During that civil war, we think he joined the rebel groups in the Ivory Coast and probably was killed in the fighting. After the war, we never heard from him again.

During this time I was teaching, I saw 9/11 happen on my own TV.

I did not date until I started my 2nd teaching job in Ghana. I had a girlfriend named Cynthia.

I had been teaching at Cambridge for about five years. Life was good.

I started looking into my old vision of joining the military. This is me: wherever I am, I am always trying to do something a little bit different, get a little bit higher than where I am. That is the vision that I see. For me, I distinguish vision and dreams separately. A vision is a different thing than a dream. I am not a dreamer. A dream is a fantasy. A dream doesn't give you the tools in the toolbox. But a vision does. A vision tells you what you need to do. You've already seen that vision, that picture, and you're working towards it. The path to getting to those pictures a vision presents you may be tough, rough, and sometimes discouraging, but you must pass through that and prevail. So that is the difference between a dream and a vision. Wherever I go, I have a vision. That vision is what I'm working towards. I've always been like that.

I was a teacher, but I wanted to be a soldier. That didn't work out because in Africa being in the military is a true profession. Only the top people, who have really good networks, are able to get in. There aren't many big wars in Africa, so they don't need that many people, and it's very competitive to get in. There is very little recruitment. The country of Ghana has an army of about 27,000 personnel. Sometimes people retire and other people move up, then they might be looking for another 50 people to join. It's very competitive to become one of those fifty people. Unless you know someone, it's unlikely that they'll bring you in. You can't just walk into it.

Winning the Lottery

Wherever I go, I always find favor from people. I believe that what my father told me is what is happening. I cannot definitively say, yes, but the fact is that wherever I go, and with the kind of attitude I approach people and my work, I always receive some form of likeness. I believe that is where it comes in. It's not an explicit reciprocal arrangement. It isn't because my father did this thing that people were kind to me. Where I live now, no one knows my father. If I see someone doing something kind for me, I think, *this might be what my father told me*.

One day, I was standing around the courtyard, and other teachers were coming up to me, saying, "Play the lottery."

They were talking about the U.S. diversity lottery, where U.S. visas were raffled off. Each year the U.S. offers so many visas to each country.

"No," I said. "I don't want to play. There's so much scam in that."

The lottery was free to enter, but I didn't think it was legitimate.

"Let's play together," a teacher said.

"No," I said. "I don't want to play."

One hundred and seven teachers in that school all played the lottery, except me. Everyone was sitting in pairs, getting their pictures taken. There was one guy left, and he wanted to sit with me, so we could get our picture together. I said, "No. I don't want my picture taken. I don't want to play this lottery."

He got upset.

They *forced* me to play. Everyone threw up their hands. "Just sit down and play this lottery," they told me. "Stop doing whatever you're doing, okay?"

"Okay, okay," I said, throwing up my own hands. "Don't eat me. I'm going to sit down and I'm going to play."

So I sat down and I played the lottery with that man. It was the end of 2001. I played the lottery, then I forgot about it.

Some weeks after that, I heard that I'd won the lottery, but I never saw proof of it. I still didn't believe the lottery was real, so I brushed these rumors aside.

Then I started hearing that people who had taken my picture were coming back looking for me. The first person they met was my best friend. They told him that I won the lottery. He told them that I no longer worked at that school. So they went back home.

I'm not sure why he did that. Maybe he was jealous. Maybe he didn't want me to leave.

A week later, they came back again. They needed to find me soon to start the process or I would run out of time to go to the U.S. They met my friend again, and again he told them the story that I'd left the school. The time was getting even shorter.

After two weeks, they came again and met a teacher named Benjamin who was not my friend. "Do you know David Dambre?" they asked.

"Yes."

"Is he in this school? Is he still teaching here?"

"Yes, he is upstairs."

"What?"

"He's upstairs."

"Okay, can you take me to him?"

This teacher took the lottery man upstairs, but unfortunately that day, I was not there. I went out to eat lunch. So he went to my classroom, and I wasn't there.

"Okay," he said. "We'll come back later."

When I returned, the teacher told me, "These guys were here looking for you. They said you won the lottery and you're going to America."

"What?" I said. "I've heard that, but I don't know it for sure."

"Well, they came. Those guys came. It's real. It's not like they're joking. They say you're going to America."

"Okay," I said. "Where are they?"

"They left. When they saw you were not here, they left. They're going to come back in a day or two."

"Thank you for telling me this."

I was hearing those whispered voices again. They were calling me across the world to America.

My friends started teasing me. "Someone has won the lottery who doesn't even know where the lottery is."

They started calling me "American, American."

Meanwhile, I didn't know where the paper was or how I won. I had no idea.

My co-workers started mocking me, "Look at this guy. He won the lottery, but he's not going to America. We don't even know where his paperwork is. We don't know *how* he won the lottery."

The next day the lottery guys didn't show up.

That school had two sites. Usually, I worked at the new site, but the next day, my proprietor came to me and said, "I know you like it here, but we want to send you to the old site because they need somebody like you there. Go and teach them, French."

"Okay," I said and I went there that day.

The following day, the lottery officials came to the school and met my friend who told them I was not there. My friend said, "I've already told you that he doesn't work here anymore."

"No," they said. "Yesterday we met someone else who said he was here. That man's name is Ben. We need to find him. Can you take us to Benjamin?"

"Okay, yeah," my friend said.

When they went to Benjamin, he said, "Well, this guy is not here, but he has been transferred to the old site. If you want to go to the old site, I can go there with you and show you where he is."

When they arrived, I was standing there preaching. It was on a Friday. Every Friday we hosted religious events. We did morning devotion, and I was the one, teaching the word of God to the students. I am a Christian, a Roman Catholic, as I had been in my village, but we didn't practice then. Then I had been triggered by the negativity of working for Mr. Appau and the way he treated me. The wife was a deaconess in the church. The way she treated me refuted the idea of "love your neighbor." Oh, hell no, it was a huge turn-off. I still felt this way: people go to church, but still, behave badly and mistreat others.

Now the belief still wasn't strong, but I was a churchgoer. I had a co-worker who was a devout Catholic, and he wanted me to go with him every Sunday.

I was standing on a platform, preaching, and we saw a Land Cruiser pull up.

Benjamin didn't tell the lottery officials that it was me speaking, so they went to my boss at the old site and said, "We're looking for Mr. Dambre."

"Why do you want to see Mr. Dambre? Are you guys police? Or investigators or something? What did he do?"

"He didn't do anything. We just want to speak with him."

My boss, being intelligent, thought maybe something was wrong because they don't know me. If they knew me, they wouldn't be asking him but would have recognized me on the podium. He told them to wait in his office."

He came over to me and whispered into my ear. "Have you done something wrong?"

"No."

"Are you sure?"

"No. I haven't done anything. I'm not a criminal. I haven't stolen anything. I didn't kill anybody. I didn't do anything."

"Well, there are two people here with that Land Cruiser looking for you. It looks like they are from the Criminal Investigation Division (CID). If you know you didn't do anything, great, I will let you go see them. But if you know you have done something, I advise that you run out of here."

"No, I didn't do anything. I want to see them."

"Okay, come see them."

I asked another teacher to take over the preaching and followed my boss back to his office.

"Hey, how are you?" they said.

"Fine."

"We don't want to talk here. Can we step outside?"

I looked at my boss.

"Okay," I said.

"Okay, Mr. Dambre, go with them," my boss said.

We went outside. The old site was in front of my house. We were standing there, and they said, "Is it you? David Dambre?"

"Yeah."

"Do you want to stand here and talk? Or do you want to go to your house? Is your house near here?

"Yes, my house is very, very far from here. We can't go to my house, but if you want to talk, we can talk from here."

"Okay," they said. "Let's go sit on that balcony over there."

That balcony was in my house!

So we went and sat down. They opened a bag and brought out a paper. They said, "Mr. Dambre, we want you to sign here to prove it's truly you."

"Uh-uh. I'm not signing. I know what a signature does. Remember, I'm a teacher. I'm not just any kind of person you ask me to sign and I just sign. What do you want to use that signature for?"

"No, you just sign. It's okay. You just sign."

I prayed in my head. *Lord, let me sign. You know I didn't do anything. If there's something I have done, you will get me out of this. If not, then let them have me.* So I signed.

As soon as I finished signing, they said, "Yep, that's you!"

I threw up my hands. "Wait. What do you mean that's me?"

"Well, you are the one who won the lottery."

I sucked in my breath and leaned way back in my chair. "What?"

They took out the letter from the U.S. immigration office and showed it to me. "Congratulations. You won the lottery."

I couldn't believe it, out of one hundred and seven teachers, I was the only one who won the lottery.

Before I could take this in, they went on, "Now you need to process everything and do this paperwork and you can go to America."

I still could hardly take this in. Even though I'd heard people were looking for me, I didn't believe it. Before I had my picture taken, I didn't even believe the lottery was real but thought it was a scam. And I couldn't understand why they had been asking so many other people, rather than coming to me directly.

After they showed me the letter, they said, "You've won the lottery and you have a month left to get processed. Or else you're going to lose this."

"Whoa," I said. I could feel my face wrinkle in confusion. "What am I supposed to do?"

"Well, you need to begin the process. This letter states the date you need to report to the embassy. You need to take a medical exam."

I had no passport. What the heck was I supposed to do?

They told me I had to get a passport on the spot. I had two days to get it. This was possible in Ghana.

They told me it was going to cost 500,000 cedis. Then there would be other payments down the line: physicals and other payments. All in all, I would need six thousand U. S. dollars just to get the visa, and then there would be a plane ticket to buy.

"But I don't have any money," I said. *Yes, I was thinking, I had my good salary at Cambridge and my tutoring money, but Cedis didn't convert into dollars. Even with the good money, I was making in Ghana, compared to six thousand U.S. dollars – it was nothing.*

"No, no, no, no, no," the guy told me. "There's somebody who is going to pay for it."

"Who is that person?"

"There's a woman who is going to sponsor you to go."

"Okay?" I said. "Just like that? Sponsor me for free?"

"She knows what she's getting out of it."

"Okay. Cool."

I saw this woman as a gift from God. I was a teacher, not making that much money to pay visa processing fees and $1,500 for a plane ticket to the U.S. This was another one of those karmic gifts: I needed a sponsor, and one appeared.

They left me with her phone number. "Call her, and the next day she will be here."

I didn't even think about why the woman would be sponsoring me. My excitement was so strong that I didn't question anything. Whatever could take me to America, I would say yes to it. I went right home and called the woman, whose name was Mary.

That night I couldn't sleep. All I kept hearing were the words, "David, you've won the lottery." I was thinking, *Me? I'm going to America? I mean, come on: I've only seen America in movies.* I've seen movies about people in New York City, with huge, tall buildings. I kept seeing the images of those buildings and thinking, *I'm going to this country? This is like a dream come true.*

I could see that my dream of getting into the military in Africa was never going to happen. So, I thought, *Okay. Let me go to America then. Let me see what is possible there.*

Cynthia and I had been dating for almost two years. She was planning on marrying me, but I wasn't quite ready.

When I won the lottery, I didn't tell her. If I had told her, one way or the other, she probably would have blocked me from going or she would have insisted that she go along, but I didn't have the money for myself, let alone both of us. I planned to go alone, earn some money, and send for her.

My excitement about going to America was so great that I started telling my friends and the other teachers at my school, but I didn't tell my family in Togo.

"Hey," I told my coworkers. "I won the lottery. I'm going to become an American."

By the way, they were talking to me, I didn't think it would take long to get money to bring Cynthia over.

"You just have to get to America," people said. "Then the American Government will get you a job and a house. You won't have to suffer. You'll have work ready for you. You'll have so much money, you'll be able to do anything you want."

I could see the green pastures. I would be making millions of dollars. Money would be growing on trees. I would just climb the trees and pluck the money, the way I'd picked those two unripe mangoes back at Pax International School.

I kept telling my friends, "Hey, I'm going to be an American."

One guy I met had come from New York to Ghana. He told me a story. "Look, man, if you're going to go to America, don't go anywhere but the Bronx, man."

After I heard that, the Bronx was on my mind all the time. I thought those big, tall buildings I'd seen in the movie were found in the Bronx. Whenever anyone asked where I was going, I would say, "I'm going to the Bronx, man. I'm going to the Bronx."

I thought the Bronx was emblematic of everything America could offer. I walked around thinking, *The Bronx, The Bronx, The Bronx, The Bronx, The Bronx.*

One day I told some of my students, "Hey, I am going to America."

They said, "Nooo."

One said, "I want you to go to Atlanta, sir." He put his hands in a prayer position. "Go to Atlanta, Georgia because my mother is there."

Another one said, "Go to Massachusetts. That's where my father is."

"You guys don't know anything," I said. "I am going to *the Bronx.* The Bronx is the best place to be."

My friend who told me about the Bronx took a picture of all his American dollars laid out on his bed and showed it to me. I saw dollars and thought it must be a lot of money.

My students started calling me "American, American."

Excitement was building all around me.

I worked at the Cambridge International School for five years.

While I was getting my paperwork together to go to the U.S., I started teaching at El Shaddai International School. Within the three months I worked there, I transformed that school. There were so many things they were not doing, but when I went in there, I really changed the whole school, and my parents were really, really happy that things were changing, but then they were also sad that I was leaving them shortly.

My school threw a big party for me. They gave me 150,000 cedis. It was awesome.

Sponsorship and Corruption

Mary came from Accra, the capital city. She called me from her hotel in Kumasi and asked me to meet her in the lobby. The first thing I noticed about her was that she was a very beautiful young woman.

"Okay," Mary said, "Since you don't have your passport, I'm going to put the passport through for you quickly. Two or three days."

Whoa, I thought. We stepped right out of the hotel and hurried over to the passport office to get my passport done.

While we waited through the different steps, Mary told me she had an uncle living in America who was sending her money. She struck me as being from an affluent family and looked like she took really good care of herself.

Before I could think too much about things, my passport was complete. *I've got a passport. So, really, I'm going to America?* It felt surreal for me just to think about it.

Mary paid the passport fees, and we walked out of the passport office.

I thought Mary was a high-class, high-maintenance girl. She was not like the kind of girls I had dated who had simpler tastes. The vibe she was putting off with the shoes she was wearing, her jeans, her top, her earrings, the bag she was carrying, and how she held herself, all told me she was looking for a high-class man who could support her in the style in which she was accustomed.

Despite her fashionable attire, she seemed to be a down-to-earth person. She was easy to talk to, and she was constantly buying me what I needed. Every morning she would meet me, and we would go do what we needed to do. She knew everything I had to do, and I didn't know anything.

"Now," Mary said. "You've got to go for your medical checkup in Accra. I'm going to have to go with you. I'm going to buy the bus ticket for you, and then we are going to go together to your medical exam. Once we get that done, you're going to have an interview at the embassy."

We took the bus to Accra. It was my first time visiting the city. Accra was so big and even more beautiful than Kumasi. It was so crowded with people. There's no space to walk, and the traffic is very congested. People were constantly bumping into each other, without even saying, "Excuse me." I wasn't a big fan, besides that, all my excitement was going to see those big tall buildings in the U.S. that I'd seen in the movies. I was going to *The Bronx*.

After two days in Accra, we went to the U.S. Embassy. We went in, she paid all the money, and then I did my check-up. They wanted to make sure I didn't have HIV/AIDS, meningitis, Hepatitis A, B, or C, or any other infectious diseases that could be brought to the U.S. The woman paid for everything.

After we left the embassy, we went to stay at Mary's auntie's house.

I passed my medical exam and a few days later I received another letter from the U.S. embassy stating that my interview had been scheduled for one week. I had to arrive early because the line at the U.S. Embassy in Ghana is crazy. If your appointment is at 5:00 pm, you need to be in the line at 5:00 am.

When we arrived, we found this long line and everyone pushing each other, fighting, saying, "I was there before you."

Another person would say, "no."

Then they would fight and beat each other up.

We went there at 5:00 am for our 4:00 pm appointment. We stood in line all day. There was nothing to do but just stand there. If somebody talked to us, we would respond, but then we would get tired. We couldn't talk for twelve hours straight. Everyone was so focused on standing in this line, waiting for their chance to go to America. No one wanted to do anything to jeopardize their chance. If you have to pee, you have to get the person in front and behind to hold your place. If you don't tell anyone, you're not getting back in line. Some older people brought their own chairs so they could sit down while they waited.

Luckily, Mary and I were there together, and we could take turns waiting in line. At one point, I was waiting, and she went off to buy some food. While she was gone, she paged me, "There's someone looking at you."

I looked up and saw a middle-aged man, walking up and down the line, studying the people in line. His eyes fell on me, and I looked away.

"Who is it?" I wrote back.

"Member of parliament."

The last time the official came out with a list, he said, "After this person here, you'll need to go back, and we'll send you another appointment."

I was the one who was going to go next, and they cut my line off. They gave us a yellow paper and said, "go home and come back in two days' time." That meant I had to stay in Accra. I was still teaching in Kumasi, but I didn't have time to go back and forth, so I stayed in Accra.

I knew I was lucky I hadn't been given a pink slip. When you get a pink slip, your chances of getting a visa are very, very tiny. A pink slip means, "Don't spend any more money. Go home."

I stayed at Mary's auntie's house. We cooked food, and we ate. We were all having fun thinking about America. While we were staying there, Mary's uncle would call us. Because of the time difference, he would call in the middle of the night.

We'd be sleeping, and the next thing I'd hear was Mary saying, "Hey, hey, uncle wants to talk to us."

I'd be rubbing my eyes, trying to figure out what was happening. It would be 4:00 am. We would talk, talk, talk, talk, talk, and then he'd say, "Go back to sleep."

The day of our appointment came, and we went back to the embassy for the interview. There were so many people, but I had a yellow paper so I didn't have to wait that long.

The official said, "All people who have their yellow paper, come forward."

I advanced where he directed.

Then, a white lady called me to her window to interview me. "David Dambre!" The sign said her name was Margaret.

I went to the little window and I stood there.

She looked at my face and said, "You're a good man."

"What do you mean?"

"I don't know," she said. "You just came in here, but I can see that you're a good man."

She looked at my certificate, which was in French. Then she began speaking to me in French. She told me her story, how she went to school in France. I told her my story, how I went to school in Togo.

"You know what," she said. "You're a good man." Then she stamped my visa paperwork. "You're going to do great stuff."

She didn't know me from anywhere. The words she was saying about me surprised me. How do you know *me*? I wondered. I've never spoken with you, but you just said I'm a good man and I'm going to do good stuff. I praised God.

I got the paperwork stamped, but there was an administrative detail left before I would get the visa itself.

"Go home," Margaret said. "And come back tomorrow. When you come back, don't wait in line. Come straight inside." She handed me a green paper. "Give this to them, they're going to let you come straight inside to my window."

I nodded. "Okay."

The next day I went back, and she gave me the actual visa.

This is when things started to get complicated. Mary stepped inside and said, "Look, somebody wants to take that visa away from you."

I was just standing there, holding the visa between my fingers for the first time. "What do you mean somebody wants to take it away from me?"

"There is a member of parliament who has to be paid $6,000 US dollars," Mary told me.

I had heard a rumor about this before our trip, but I didn't know any details. Somebody had whispered, "If you win it, watch out," and mentioned an official's name, but I hadn't paid too much attention.

"I paid him some of the money," Mary went on, "But not all of it. He said he's going to take your visa until he gets all his money. If we give him any more money, we won't have enough for our plane tickets."

"Wait a minute, Mary," I said. "This is a member of parliament doing this? This is the man you paged me about?"

"Yes," she said. "His name is Ken, and he goes around running this lottery program. Honorable Ken Agyapong as he is popularly known is a current Member of Parliament of Assin North. He was first elected a member of parliament in 2000 to the seat of Assin North. He takes people's pictures and fills out the paperwork, then sends in the application. Then whoever wins has to pay him $6,000 US dollars."

I threw up my hands. Now I knew why the lottery officials came looking for me over and over again as they were concerned about running out of time: They were worried they wouldn't get their part of the $6,000.

"Once we pay that, it's not guaranteed you're going to get the visa to go to America. If you don't get it, you lose the $6,000. When you go for an interview, you have to pay for the physical exam, and the visa itself, which is another $2,000-3000 US dollars. After all that you still may not get to come to the US. Now you've sold everything you have, chasing this visa."

Everything Mary was saying was going too fast. I couldn't think it through. "But I have my visa," I said, holding it between my fingers.

"Right now, you do. But we need to find somebody we trust inside the embassy that can take that visa and walk out with it so you can walk out empty-handed. Because Ken is standing outside on those steps waiting for you to come out."

I could see my dream of reaching those tall buildings in the Bronx fading away. Was this really true? This man who had encouraged me to play the lottery was now forcing me to pay for this visa or give it up?

But Mary had it all figured out. "When we go outside, you'll tell him that you didn't get it today and will get it another day. Then we'll walk away, and he will not see you anymore."

We looked around for someone we could give the visa to and found somebody she knew. She spoke to the guy and slipped the visa inside his package, and he walked out with it. I was missing the feel of that visa between my fingers, but I wasn't too worried about losing it. The visa had my name on it, and Mary and this guy could not pretend to be me. If he took it to immigration, he would not be able to answer questions to prove he was me. I was much less afraid of this transaction than it was of Ken.

"Good plan," I said.

When Mary and I walked out, Ken was standing there at the door.

"Hey," he said to me. "Give me that visa."

"They didn't give it to me today," I said. "Margaret said I should come back in two days."

He shook his head at me. "No. You're lying. I knew they were going to give the visa to you today."

"How did you know that the embassy would give the visa today?" I asked.

"Don't play that game with me. I knew they were going to give it to you. Either you give me that visa now or you're not going to America."

He didn't mention that he needed to be paid more money, but I knew that from Mary.

"Sir, I don't have it now. Maybe tomorrow or two days' time when I come back, I will get it and give it to you."

"No." He gathered five big boys by his side. "You see these guys here? If you don't give me the visa, they're going to beat you up."

"Sir? You know that I'm a teacher, right? I know my rights. I know what I can do, and I know what I cannot do. If *you* make a mistake and you hit me, you will go to jail."

He scowled at me. "You're just a teacher. A simple teacher. You are nobody. And you're going to stand here and tell me you're a teacher?"

"Okay, this is where I'm going to tell you I'm a teacher. Do you know that under international law, if you are a government official of a certain country, you're not supposed to interfere with anything relating to another government?"

"Whoa!" he said. He looked at me from the corner of his eye. "Who told you that?"

"Oh? So, you thought I didn't know?"

He pulled back, awake now. "Boys," he said to the five big guys. "Stand down." I could see the look on his face as he realized that I could get him into trouble.

"If you don't know, if you beat me or you ask those guys to beat me up, I am going inside the embassy and I'm going to tell them who you are and what you're doing besides your official government duties."

He tilted his head and looked at me. "You know what, I'm going to let you go. I'm not going to do anything to you but remember this." He pointed his finger at me. "When you get to the airport, to fly out, immigration is going to stop you, because I will tell them to stop you."

"Okay. Let them stop me. If they stop me, because you told them to, I know what to tell them. I will explain to them what your job is, how you ask for this $6,000, and how it is against international law. So, are you going to ask them to stop me from going or do you want to go to jail because if someone finds out, the United States government can arrest you and the Ghanaian government can jail you for doing this kind of job?"

He scratched his head. "Wow. Okay." He waved me off. "You go and see. At the airport, you'll see."

"Fine. Let me get to the airport, and when they kick me back, I'll call you and say, 'Ken, you have done a good job. You kicked me out. That's fine.' But let me go."

So, I went.

Mary and I walked away from him and didn't look back. It wasn't until we walked away from that I saw my hands were shaking from the encounter. Even though I'd acted confidently and stood my ground, I'd also been scared.

Later that night, we met up with the man who had my visa, and he gave it back to me.

We scheduled our flight for one week away on November 7, 2002. I went home to pack my things. After I got home from Accra, Kumasi seemed like a village to me.

Now that I was really going to the U.S., I had to break the news to Cynthia.

I was able to calmly explain it to her. "Look, let me go, and when I go, I will get money and come back for you."

Cynthia cried, but in the end, agreed with the plan.

4

Indentured in America

Cynthia came to Accra with me so she could escort me to the airport.

The night before I left for the United States, I could not sleep. The thought of going, the thought of traveling, the thought of being on the plane, and the thought of getting to where I wanted to be, were dominating my thoughts to the point that it was impossible for me to sleep.

I thought back to the night before I left for Ghana, that first step in my journey, how that rooster kept waking me up. There was no rooster to rely on in Accra. We didn't have to get up early in the morning because we left Accra around 11 PM. We had the whole day to spend sleeping and eating. Mary's family cooked a big feast. We sat there and ate.

On November 7, 2002, one of Mary's brothers drove Cynthia, Mary, and me to the airport. Mary had the tickets her uncle had purchased for us inside her handbag.

It was my first time flying. I had seen planes flying by from a distance, but I'd never been up close to one to see how big they were. I expected them to be much smaller than they were, but they were huge. *How can these huge things be sent in the air*? I wondered.

At the airport, I was looking all around me, while still trying to play it cool. I was looking for anyone saying, "Hey, you're not going anywhere." Nobody said anything to me, so we proceeded through the airport to the gate.

Then Cynthia was hugging me and didn't want to let go.

"It won't be long before I'm back," I said. "I'll marry you and take you back to the U.S. with me."

Cynthia finally let go, and Mary and I boarded the plane. I had a lot of worries as we took off. My mind, all whole thoughts were full of flying, being in this thing that was taking me into the sky. Anything could happen. What if something happens and it falls? Then what will happen to us? The part that scared the hell out of me was when we got into some turbulence. We were hitting the snow. *Oh, Lord have Mercy.* I almost screamed out loud. We were shaking from side to side. *Are we going down? Lord*, I was praying. *We can't die here. I need to go and make some money and go take care of my family.* That was all I cared about at that point. I didn't have time to die. Even if the plane fell out of the sky, I couldn't die because I had to get to America and make money and take care of my family. That was my mindset.

We first touched down in Zurich, Switzerland then switched planes and landed at Washington Dulles Airport. My first impression was the lights, the streetlights. When the plane was descending, I saw all the streetlights and the city lights. *Yes!* I thought. *This is where I'm going to be.*

But when I got down, I wondered where the lights were. From the sky, they had looked so close to each other, but on the ground, they were more spread out.

I was still afraid that immigration might try to stop me because I was still afraid of all that parliament members had said to me. But nobody stopped me. They said, "Welcome to America."

"Thank you!" I said and that was it.

We filled out all our paperwork.

Then we stepped out of the airport. My first impression was the snow. It was a big, big, big, big, big snow. It was the heaviest snow.

I was starstruck. I was confused. *Yep*, I said. *I got here. This is money's home. This is where I'm going to be.*

"Hey, Mary?" I asked. "Where is the Bronx?"

She puzzled up her face. "The Bronx? Who's going to take you to the Bronx? The Bronx is not the best place."

"What? Aren't we going to the Bronx?"

"No, hell no, we're not going there."

"So where are we going?"

"We're going to Maryland," she said.

Then we took a cab to her uncle's house in Hyattsville, Maryland. Along the way, my first impressions matched what I'd dreamed of and what I'd seen in the movies. It was real. It was no longer the movies, it was reality. I took a deep breath and thought, *This is where my journey leads. I'm going to make a lot of money and go back home and build a big house for my family in Togo.*

"Welcome to America!" the uncle called out when we walked in with our bags.

"Hey, welcome," said his wife.

"You guys did it," the uncle said.

After a week I got my social security card.

The uncle said, "Okay, guys, we're having a family meeting."

I had a sinking feeling, but I said, "Okay," and sat down at the dining room table with the uncle, the aunt, and the woman.

"Hey," the uncle said. "A lot of money was sent to you. You were spending everything, the $6,000 for the member of parliament, the airfare. We've calculated everything and it was about $10,000. So, you'll have to pay for it."

"What do you mean, I have to pay?" I said. I was just sitting there, unable to believe this was happening to me. My brother had taken me to Ghana and tricked me into working in slavery for the old man for a year, and now, after seven years of having my life together, of supporting myself as a French teacher and sending money to my family in Togo, this woman Mary has tricked me into becoming an indentured servant to her uncle. How did I *get* here?

I tried again. "Nobody said it was a loan you were giving to me. I was told you were sponsoring me. Not that I would have to pay you back. There is nothing written down on paper that shows I owe you money. You didn't even mention this to me. All you told me was that the member of parliament was taking $6,000, and you paid him. So, why now, are you telling me to pay?"

I said all of this very calmly. You have to have options to grow wings, but I didn't have options. My thought was *if I say no, the mood in the house would not be okay. There's going to be a fight. So, I'm just going to pretend that I'm agreeing to it until I find my own way out. Once I find my own way out, then I can begin to let him know what I'm thinking.*

I stayed calm because I did not want to get hit, he and his wife jinxed up and started fighting me and had them tell me to get out. *If they told me to get out, where was I supposed to go?*

"Well," the uncle said. "That was the deal. We paid him, now you pay us. If you don't pay us, you'll go to jail."

I stared across the table at Mary, my so-called sponsor. Little did I know all the time she was helping me that she too had a cut in it too. Now I knew she didn't give the MP all the money because she wanted her part of the money. She tricked him, but the uncle still wanted me to pay the full amount. They were using me as a money machine.

When I woke up to that, I decided I wasn't going to pay that money.

At this point, I was wishing I'd never won the lottery and was just back in Ghana teaching at El Shaddai International School.

I shook my head. "I'm not going to jail," I told him. "I will never, never, never, never, never go to jail. There is nothing to prove you loaned this money to me. You didn't explain it to me. You didn't tell me about it or anything. I told you guys I didn't have money and you said 'oh no, don't worry. Everything will be taken care of.' So now you're telling me to pay. No. I don't have money."

"That's a funny joke, David," the uncle said.

His wife pretended to laugh.

I just stared at them in disbelief.

I had swallowed so many things to get to where I wanted to be, I wasn't going to spoil it now. I told myself, *I'm almost there, I can hold on and take care of myself until I get to where I really want to be my final destination.* I thought about my journey. *I've gone through all this. The old man and his wife treated me so badly, but I made it through that. I was able to handle it. I made my own way in Ghana and started working as a teacher. Now that I'm here, I'm not going to mess this up. I'm going to wait until everything goes the way I want it.*

They were still staring across the table at me, expecting me to produce

$10,000 dollars.

I could see no way out of this, so I told them, "I will pay." But I didn't really mean it.

That night I lay in bed, really starting to think about where I'd landed.

I remembered all my excitement back in Kumasi, learning that I'd won the lottery and that Mary was going to sponsor me. Never did I ask myself, *who is she and why is she sponsoring me?* I hadn't even thought, *she doesn't know me: All of a sudden, she wants to sponsor me to go to America?*

I knew that even if I had thought about it, I wouldn't have cared, as long as she took me to America, I was ready to go.

Things were not working out the way I had hoped with Cynthia. I couldn't get the money to go back and get her. It wasn't at all the way I'd heard in Ghana. The American Government wasn't getting me a job, much less a house. I was on my own to figure it out.

I felt tricked the way I had when my brother came from Kumasi to my home village, wearing those fine clothes, and I decided to go back to Ghana with him, only to find out, he was selling me into slavery. Well, now I'd been tricked again, only this time I was indentured in America.

Mary had led me into this situation, the way my brother in Togo had led me into slavery. I thought of all the times I had trusted her and did what she said. I remembered that tense moment in the embassy when she told me that Honorable Kenneth Agyapong was demanding $6,000 for my visa, and she couldn't pay him all the money. Then we gave the visa to a man she knew in the embassy. She had planned all that in advance. Now I imagined she had planted that man there, paid him his cut to smuggle out my visa, so she could keep the money Ken wanted from us.

"That Is Your Patient"

My uncle and aunt found me a job as a certified nursing assistant (CNA). One of their friends was working in the J B Johnson Nursing Home in DC. The nursing home sponsors people who pass tests, and they pay for your training, then you go and get your certification and license, and go back and work for them. After six months, you're free to work somewhere else.

I went and took the test. *Another test*, I thought. *I'd been taking tests all my life*. Like all the others, I passed. The nursing home paid for all my training and gave me a biweekly paycheck. *Okay, good*, I thought. *I'm getting there. I'm about to live the American dream.*

After living with the uncle for six months, I went to live with his son who had an apartment in Enfield Court. I moved into the son's apartment and started paying half the rent. That is when I finally felt free enough to confront the uncle. "Hey, I said, "I am not going to pay the money because you guys didn't tell me."

The uncle did not let it go. "You owe me that money. Once you start working, you will pay me back."

But I was out of his house and already I felt better. And I think that me paying half his son's rent made him feel I was contributing something to his family.

I took the CNA class at VMT Educational Center, opposite the University of the District of Columbia. I would take the train from Carleton, switch at Union Station, get off at Van Ness Station, and walk to the school. While I was walking, I would stare at the impressive university buildings. I had a dream that someday I would go to a university.

In the training, I learned what the CAN job entailed, and what was awaiting me. When I took my practical, we were feeding residents, but that was our only responsibility.

In September 2003 I passed the course, and I started my job.

I found out that being a CNA involved more than just feeding elderly people: I was expected to wipe them, dress them, and bathe them. I hadn't known that being a CNA would be that kind of work. Coming from a conservative, isolated culture, I thought, *No way. I am not going to do this kind of job.*

On my first day at work, the nurse practitioner said, "You have nine patients."

What I didn't realize right away, was that five of those patients were females, and four were males.

Unfortunately for me, in the very first room I went in, I found a female. I ran out of the room and found the nurse practitioner. "Hey! There's a woman in there."

"What?" she said.

I pointed back to the room. "There's a woman in there."

"Yeah. That is your patient."

"What do you mean that's my patient? How? I'm a *man*. How am I supposed to take care of a *woman*?"

"Sir. That is your patient. If you don't take care of her, the patient's family is going to sue you. Also, you will be fired and need to pay back all the money for your training."

I shook my head to clear my thoughts. *Was I dreaming or was this real?* I had just come from Africa, and in Africa, men are separated from women. It would never occur to me that I could care for a female patient.

"Sir," my boss said. "Are you going to do the job we're paying you to do?"

"Okay," I said. "I will do it."

I worked for two weeks. Then I resigned. I just couldn't do it. The culture was so different that I *could not* get out of that bubble.

Joining the U.S. Army

During the two weeks working at the nursing home, I met a guy from Kenya named Simon who was working there as a part-time CNA. We started having conversations, while we were both working the same shift, and I made a good relationship with him.

I asked Simon if he knew anyone who was in the army.

He pointed his finger toward another coworker who was sitting across from Simon and me.

I asked, are you in the army?

"I'm in the Army Reserves, replied."

"You're in the military?" I asked. "I've been wanting to go to the military. What did you do to get there?"

"Are you sure?"

"Yeah."

"Okay." He clapped his fist into his other hand. "I will give you somebody's number and you will call."

That was during the time the war was raging in Iraq, but I wasn't going to let that stop me. I had been wanting to be in the military since my early teens.

So, when Simon told me I had a chance to join the military, I was like, *Yes! This is a great opportunity for me.*

I called the number, and they were very quick to snap me up. This was nothing like in Africa. The U.S. was at war: they needed people.

The recruiter I spoke to was named Sergeant Turner. He came to meet me and said, "We want you to take a quick practice test and see if you pass this. Then you can go take the real test."

Here we go again, I thought. *Another test.* I passed the practice test with flying colors.

"You know what," he said, chuckling. "I don't think you need the real test."

He sent my test to the center and said, "You're qualified. You need to come in for processing."

The only person who knew I was joining the military was my Kenyan friend.

"Hey, Simon," I said, the next time we were working. "I'm joining the military."

"What? Have you thought about it?"

"I've already signed up."

"What?"

"Yep."

"Don't you know there's a war going on in Iraq right now? They're going to send you to war."

I shrugged my shoulders. "I don't care. I just want to go. I wanted to join the military back home, but I couldn't get in."

The only problem was the nursing home was upset because they had paid for my certificate, and now I was going to quit.

"Hey, guys," I told them. "I'm joining the military."

"Okay," the administrator said, throwing her hands up. "If you want to join the military, we cannot stop you. We don't want to have any fight with Uncle Sam, so go ahead. For all the things you needed to pay for, we're going to waive those fees. In fact, we have a paycheck coming for you."

"Okay, thank you."

They gave me the check, and I went.

In October 2003, almost a year since I had come to the U.S., the army shipped me out for basic training. They wouldn't tell me where they were sending me.

I didn't tell the uncle's son I was going to the military until I was about to head out.

The recruiter came and parked in the parking lot. He called me and said, "Come out."

That's when I packed my stuff. "Hey," I said to the son. "I'm going to the military."

"What?"

"I'm leaving today."

I gave him my rent money. All the time I was in training to be a CNA, I was collecting a paycheck, so I could pay the rent. I found out later he never paid the rent, just spent the money I gave him, and eventually got kicked out.

I didn't even know where I was going for basic training. Even as we boarded the bus and started riding there, we weren't allowed to see the road. The drill sergeant would order us to put our heads on the seats in front of us so we couldn't see anything, and we obeyed. When we stopped at a rest stop, sure, we saw the signs of the area where we'd stopped, but they thought that if we knew the route to where we were going, we might try to run away, so on the bus, they wouldn't let us see anything. It was mind manipulation more than anything. It was the first step of breaking us down and remolding us as the soldiers they wanted us to be.

All this time riding the bus, with my head bumping against the seat in front of me, I had a lot of time to think about my journey so far.

When I came to the United States, my family didn't know I was alive until I called them and told them I was in America.

Whenever I want to do anything critical, I don't tell anyone. And I have a reason. My reason is this: Where I come from, people hate each other for whatever reason, and when you tell them what you want to *do*, they may kill you. They believe in voodoo. Where I come from, the whole village believes in voodoo, even though there is some Christianity, Christianity doesn't mean anything to them. It's like a symbol only. The majority of people are Muslim or have no religious affiliation. Everything they do, they believe in those small gods, they worship, they kill, they slaughter goats and chicken to worship these things to protect them. They can use that to kill you, to hurt you, to affect you. They could try to stop you from getting a job.

A friend I'd met from the Ivory Coast who now lives in the U.S. had told me a story about how he could not get a job despite being qualified. He was called for interviews, sent a letter of acceptance, then they picked someone else. He believed some witches or voodoo people were trying to prevent him from progressing. Where I come from, those things exist. People use witchcraft. There is witchcraft everywhere. Some people use it for good things, other people use it to do bad things.

I believe that things like that happened to my brothers, but not me personally. One of my brothers died prematurely, the way my father did. Another brother and a sister also died young. So I believe those things happen, however, personally I think I'm a different kind of breed because God has a different way of keeping me safe and protecting me from this mindset. I used to believe in voodoo, but now I don't believe in it. And if you're not believing in it, and not associated with it, they no longer have a way of getting to you. If you're in the same environment it might happen to you, but I don't believe that it can cross oceans to get to where you are.

So, if you tell someone your plans, they may try to go to a voodoo person and try to stop you from progressing. I believe this because I was there in that situation, so I don't tell anybody what I'm going to do.

When I was coming to America, I didn't tell my family. When I joined the military, I did not tell them. So no one knew where I was at that moment in time as I hurtled down some highway with my head against the seat in front of me, towards a destination I did not know.

I had time to think about how families are together: when you succeed it's for the entire family, when you fail, it's for you personally. In the village, where I come from, these people – people are progressing, but they're really standing still. When they see you coming as in competition, they kill you, but they stay where they are. You're going to think they're rich. That's what happened to the guy who wouldn't loan me his bicycle. He was doing well for himself. In our house, we weren't. Instead of helping me, he was saying the bicycle money is in my stomach. How is that supposed to help me? They take the lead and press the other people down. That's the kind of life it was. Everybody was suspicious about things. There was no free thinking.

In America, I was learning that we think independently, and we focus on the nuclear family. But Togo had been colonized by the French. We didn't want to take risks, we didn't want to venture into scary things for fear that we might fail and for fear that we'll get stuck somewhere and won't have anyone to come in and rescue us.

In the U.S., kids were learning the distal parental system, which espouses children to take responsibility for their actions and to think independently. But as a colonized country, in Togo, I grew up with the proximal parental style, which espouses people to be dependent, not think, and not take risks.

When Africans are watching white people do surfing and other adventurous sports, we are standing there saying, *how crazy to be doing that. Maybe they're going to die*. We are not raised to think independently.

Wherever we were born, we just want to stay there and not go out of our comfort zone. But that wasn't what I did. I crossed that line, and that's the story I wanted to tell.

"You Will Sing the National Anthem"

When I arrived at basic training, I found out I'd landed in Jackson, South Carolina.

Another thing I found out right away was that I was losing all track of Cynthia. There was no way I could make an international call from that base, so I lost all track of her and our plans for me to go back and bring her to the U.S. As more and more time went by, it became impossible to keep up with the long-distance relationship. That's how our communication was cut off.

When I joined the army, I could still remember back to those songs we sang at my village school, especially the military march.

I went through all the processes and to the unit where I was going to train. I learned that when you first join the military, they break you down first. Then later they remold you into what they want you to be. However, the culture I was from and the military culture crashed so badly. It was like the cultural crash I experienced as a CNA.

The very first thing I learned was how to respect the drill sergeant. Those words were pounded into my head: drill sergeant, drill sergeant, drill sergeant, drill sergeant, drill sergeant. Every morning we would wake up and do some running.

One day my drill sergeant came to me and told me something I'd done wrong.

I had a problem with the language. That's where the cultures crashed. The way they spoke, especially the military jargon, alluded me. They could not understand my accent. My accent was purely African. The way Americans pronounce their words is so slippery that often they were saying things I didn't understand. Being in the military you can't waste time trying to figure out what they want you to do. They speak once, and you're to follow their orders. But for me, I had to sit down for one or two minutes to try to understand what they wanted me to do.

I smiled at the drill sergeant. Smiling for me meant I recognized I'd made a mistake so I would correct it, and I smiled at her because I didn't want to appear rude.

But when I smiled, the drill sergeant said, "What are you *smiling* at?"

That was my biggest mistake. I threw my hands in the air. "Drill sergeant, I'm not smiling at you."

"Are you speaking to me?" she asked.

"Yes."

"Oh no. Now he's speaking to *me*." Then, she asked me, "Do I look pretty to you?"

Instead of just shutting my mouth, I said, "Yes. You look pretty."

Oh, boy. Now she called five other drill sergeants around me. Now I had to do a whole bunch of push-ups. I started sweating. Finally, I could do no more push-ups.

I tried to explain to them that I didn't understand what they were saying.

"It's not like I don't want to do what you want me to do. It takes me time to understand what you want me to do. By the time I figured it out, the other soldiers had carried out the order. I have to take my time and watch what they're doing so I can do the same thing."

"Then you shouldn't have joined," one of the sergeants said.

I felt my eyes roll wildly in surprise. "Okay?" I was thinking, *You guys wanted me.* The Iraq War was raging, and they wanted people. They wanted people so quick.

"You know what," one of the sergeants told me. "You have about two days until you're going to sing the National Anthem for us."

I shook my head in surprise. I had no idea how to sing the American National Anthem. The only song that was in my head was "Marché, Marché, Marché."

It took me two days to learn how to sing the National Anthem.

I went and told my drill sergeant, "I'm ready to sing the National Anthem."

"No," she said. "They're giving you three days."

"Drill sergeant," I said. "I'm ready to sing. *Now.*"

"We gave you three days," she said.

"I don't want the three days. I want to sing it now. I want to show you that I can do it."

"Okay," she said and grouped all the soldiers in formation. All of the platoons came. Then they called me to step forward and sing the American National Anthem.

I sang it perfectly for them.

"Wow," my sergeant said.

I was currently a Private II and after that, I was advanced to Private III. My sergeant came to me and pinned me with my new badge.

"You know what," she said. "You just got a promotion. Many of the American soldiers standing around you cannot sing the National Anthem like that. You made us proud."

Freezing in South Korea

When I reached Basic Training, the uncle who had sponsored me didn't even know which state I was in. I finished my Basic Training and went back to my uncle's place, just to let him know I was in the military and that I would be leaving again soon.

That was when he and his wife really started to insist that I pay back the

$10,000. They thought that because I was in the military, I had money.

That's when I told them I was not going to pay them.

"You have to pay the money," they argued.

"Nope," I said. "I'm not going to pay the money. Because you guys were not clear with me. I'm not sure why it happened the way it happened, but I just say that it is God who brought you guys my way. And I want to thank you guys for helping me."

"Uh, no," they said. "You gotta pay. Ten thousand dollars, you gotta pay."

I threw up my hands. "I'm in the military." And that was it.

I wanted them to understand that it was not okay to do things the way they did. They should have explained the plan to me and let me decide if I even wanted to go to America, much less work off $10,000 worth of debt to them.

If I had stayed behind in Ghana, working as a French teacher, I would have become rich.

Meanwhile, the military gave me a Military Occupational Specialty (MOS), which in my case was a supply. My title was Unit Supply Specialist. I ordered supplies, picked them up, distributed and assigned them to soldiers. If soldiers lost their supplies, I charged them and ordered new ones. Basically, it was my job to make sure everyone had food and equipment.

Each job had a code. For example, 92-Alpha stood for logistics, but I was in 92- Yankee, which stood for supply.

I had to go to Fort Lee, Virginia for Advanced Individual Training (AIT). I trained there for nine weeks. Then I graduated and I was shipped out.

"I'd like to go home and see my family in Togo," I said.

"No," they said. "You're going straight to Korea. South Korea."

I didn't have the opportunity to go.

"There's no time. They need you in South Korea immediately."

"Okay!"

I flew to South Korea. Our unit was located close to North Korea. If North Korea did something wrong, our unit would be the first to respond. We were called First 15 Field Artillery. There were only men in that unit because of the environment. Every Thursday at 4 AM, we would hear horns coming from North Korea, and we would see flares. We were always ready to go to war. We would all get up and dressed and get ready to go to war.

We would go out into the field for three months at a time. While we were in the field we would sleep in our vehicles or in tents. It was frickin' cold. *Jesus Christ*! When you sneezed, everything coming out of your nose was already ice. When you went out to pee, your urine came out as ice. That close to the northern border it was really, really cold. There were two big mountains on either side of where we were living. We would not have any hot food, only cold Meal Ready to Eat (MREs).

When we were not in the field, we were living in barracks.

Like the year I had spent working for Mr. Appau, this was a very lonely time in my life. One person who made it all feel better for me was my buddy Specialist Bradley Beard. I just loved to be around him. He was funny, although before I spoke to him, I thought he might be mean. His facial expression was so stern that he looked scary, but when I grew close to him, I saw that he was the coolest guy to be with. He was a very tall, huge, gigantic guy. When I stood next to him, I looked like his son.

He was a very funny guy. He liked to talk to me about his wife and how he cared about her, how he really loved her. It was refreshing to meet someone with such a good relationship with some of the other characters I had known in Ghana, like Mr. Appau and his terrible wife and my brother who beat his wife on the cacao farm. Specialist Beard talked so much about his wife that I could tell he was a family guy.

Together we would go downrange. Every Friday we would go off post, and he would get drunk. There were clubs close to the entrance of the post, which is how the locals make money off the military.

When we went downrange, he said, "Look, you're my buddy. Since you don't drink, I will drink, and you take me back to the barracks."

He would get drunk, and I would be the responsible buddy, taking him through the gate and making sure he had his identification card.

I don't know why, but I never drank. When I went downrange, outside the military base, it would be with a sixteen-ounce water bottle sticking out of my back pocket. The other guys were trying to get me to drink and smoke, but I would just take swigs from my water bottle. I knew how to withstand peer pressure. I would walk Specialist Beard back to the base and take care of him. I'd make sure he didn't get run over crossing the street. I would help him on and off the bus.

When he would get drunk, he'd say, "Hey, Buddy, take care of me."

"I've got you," I'd say, clasping my hands together. "You drink as much as you want. I'm here for you."

That was how we built a bond between us. He trusted me with his life. He knew that no matter what happened, I would always be there. Nobody could touch him. If anything, I would be the one who knew exactly what happened to him.

One day, I told him I wanted to buy a desktop computer.

"No, no, no," he said. "You don't have to buy a whole computer. Let's go together and buy the parts. I can build a computer for you."

"Really?"

"Yeah."

We went downrange to the PX and bought all the little parts. He walked through the store saying, "This is what we need," and throwing the pieces into a shopping cart.

When we got back, he built a desktop computer for me. It was the first time I'd ever had a computer. That is how close of friends we were. He was a very good friend. We were very, very nice to each other.

When we were in the field, we wouldn't shower for all those months. In that harsh environment, there were no females in our unit. When we were in the field for three months, we wouldn't see a single woman. People would be getting depressed, getting crazy, but my friendship with the Specialist got me through all that.

We used heavy-duty weapons out there, including Bradley. The Bradley could shoot up to fifty miles. The infantry are the worst people to be with. They are the craziest people. I was in supply, working with the infantry, it was a tough environment, but Specialist Beard and I endured it together.

When we got back to the barracks, we would go out together and look at girls.

"Today, we're going downrange," he would say, clapping his hands together.

"We're going to go look for girls, man."

In the military, we did crazy things. That was how we got through it. The training was hard, it was crazy, and sometimes people smoked. They didn't smoke for fun, but to let out the stress of the environment. You had to do something to stay alive.

"Man, let's go get some girls," he would say.

It turned out those girls were from the Philippines. Their boss was a Korean. Someone had sold them from the Philippines into prostitution. We realized that by meeting with them we were contributing to a bad situation, and our military said, "You're not supposed to do this. Don't go downrange anymore. Don't go to those clubs until they change their policy."

That's how we realized the girls had been trafficked into prostitution.

Specialist Beard was genuinely funny, he wasn't faking anything. I knew that whatever he told me was true about him. He didn't know how to lie.

Every week, we'd have mail calls, and I would get so sad because I didn't have anyone to write me a letter. Every week, he'd get a letter, sometimes more than one, from his wife.

One day, we were at mail call and I was just standing around. I wasn't expecting any mail. My family in Togo didn't even know I was in the military, much less that I was in this remote area of South Korea. Then I heard the sergeant call out, "Specialist Dambre."

What? I was so surprised.

I went up and the sergeant handed me two envelopes. The first one I held up, and I recognized Mrs. Beard's handwriting. *Whoa!*

I covered one side of my mouth and whispered to Specialist Beard, "Hey, your wife wrote me a letter."

"She did?" he asked, feigning surprise.

I looked at the other letter and didn't recognize the return address but saw that the writer was from the same town as Mrs. Beard. When I opened it, I found out that she was one of Mrs. Beard's friends.

These two letters made my life really, really special.

I found out that Specialist Beard had asked his wife and her friend to write me one because he felt so bad for me. That's how close we were to each other.

Then our sister unit, 2nd Infantry 17, got a call to deploy to Iraq. Our unit, 1st 15 Field Artillery, had to support them to get everything ready to go. While 2nd 17FA was preparing to deploy, they asked for volunteers from 1st 15 FA.

I overheard Specialist Beard talking about how he was going to volunteer to go.

I told my buddy, "Look, *do not* volunteer. They're going to come for us. We're going to be *next*. No doubt about it, we're going to go. But don't volunteer yet."

"I want to go to Iraq and get more money so I can buy a new car for my wife," he said.

"Don't," I said, shaking my head. "Don't. Don't. Don't volunteer. It's coming to us. It's sitting down there in our faces. It's coming. So when the time comes, we are going next. So don't volunteer yet."

"I want to get my wife a car she really, really wants," he said. "It's a Malibu. I have to buy it for my wife."

He followed through with his decision to volunteer and transferred to Unit 217. After the training, we all transferred to 217 and helped them ship stuff to Kuwait. But when it was time to leave, he went with 217, and I stayed back.

The next month, we were at assembly in formation, and my first sergeant said, "We lost one of our soldiers. It's hard, so pray for his soul."

"Who?" somebody asked.

"Specialist Beard."

When I heard his name like that I nearly collapsed out of formation.

I couldn't even take in the details that his convoy was hit by a rocket-propelled grenade, until later.

When I heard he was gone, my life, everything, just changed completely from having fun in the military to thinking about what I'd just seen in my mind, losing this person who was so close to me, and how he went just like that, without me saying thank you or goodbye. That really changed my entire view of the military. Not in a negative way, but it made me want to do more for the military, to work in order to honor him. Even though his family didn't know me, we had been closer than anybody else.

After assembly, my first sergeant came and said, "Hey, take a week off. You can talk to people, whatever you want to do. Go out and talk to girls. Our unit doesn't have females, so go out, and do whatever you want to do for one week and don't come to work. Don't answer anything. When you hear the horns at 2:00 am, don't wake up. Just sleep. And after one week, we will see where you are."

That's how I started drinking actually. After Specialist Beard's death, I had another buddy named Mercado who was from Mexico. He didn't have his citizenship yet. Like me, he put in paperwork to become a citizen. He would go out with me.

The very first time I drank, I took a shot. For someone like me who didn't know how to drink, I could get drunk on very little. This was Korean tequila, known as Soju. *Wow*, I thought, taking that shot. *All that time I spent distilling the old man's tequila. So, this is what it tasted like!*

Oh my God. I saw myself flying like a little bird.

Mercado took me back to the gate, and there was a puddle in front of it. I thought that puddle was really big.

"Look at me," I said. "I'm going to jump into this enormous body of water."

"Okay," Mercado said. "Be careful now."

I walked back so I could get a running start for my giant leap across this lake. I ran and ran and made a long jump to cross that huge body of water. As I was jumping across, I knew I couldn't make it all the way across and I fell down into that water.

It took me a while to get better. I kept drinking. I would drink Specialist Beard's favorite kind of beer. I would drink his favorite mixed drink. In my mind, I would say, *I'm drinking for him.*

It was a really tough time. When he died, it really got to me. Even now, it still gets to me. Sometimes I sit down and I still have some issues. I can't think, can't concentrate. I can't think straight that I lost him.

After that week, I got back into the routine of military life. We were training to go to Iraq. My unit finally got orders to go. During that time, I got hurt in training. At first, I didn't know it was serious, but after a week or so my leg became very heavy, and I could not lift it anymore. I went on sick call, and they could not do anything for me.

"Hey," they said. "Go to the hospital."

The hospital was in Yongsan, South Korea. The first doctor that took care of me, Dr. Hall, had my hip scanned.

After that scan he said, "Look. Your injury is serious. You need to go back to the States and have surgery. Were you hit by a car?" he asked.

"No. I jumped over the car. During the maneuver, I was jumping with a weapon and I fell and that's probably when it happened."

"Yeah," he said, nodding his head. "This is serious. You need to go as soon as possible."

So, I couldn't go to Iraq, even though I really wanted to go. But I couldn't continue with the military.

I came back to the US in 2005, and I had two surgeries on my right hip in Kentucky at Fort Knox. Dr. Poepers, a military doctor, was the one who performed the surgery.

After he looked at it, he said, "Hey, we see some ingrown bone. So we need to go in there and cut it."

The first surgery didn't do it. Somehow, he also damaged some nerves. That contributed to the problem. So they had to do a second surgery from the other side of the hip. After that, I was a liability to my buddies and I could not do so much, so I had to leave the military.

5

Attending University

While I was recovering from surgery, I took some courses that allowed me to continue to community college. When I came out of the military in Kentucky, I moved to Maryland. I went and found my old Kenyan friend, Simon, who I'd met at the nursing home my first year in America. I stayed with him for 4-6 months and during that time a friend introduced me to a girl from Ghana who lived in Texas.

She and I talked on the phone. She told me that she was in nursing school and was going to be a nurse. Sometimes she would say, "I'm driving. I'll call you back."

I didn't have a job and wasn't doing anything, so I told Simon, "Well, I found a girl who is in Texas now. Maybe I will move down there and see if I can find a job."

The girl found me an apartment. So, in 2007 I moved to Texas.

I met the girl and we started meeting in person. I liked her, but I started wondering where the car she always drove was.

So, one day, I asked her, "Hey, where's your car that you've been driving?"

"That was my mom's car."

"Do you know how to drive?" I asked, now doubtful of everything she had told me.

She shook her head. "No."

"But you told me you were driving."

"I was lying."

"Why?"

"I don't have papers. So, I can't drive."

She wasn't a citizen, so she couldn't drive. I quickly found out she had lied to me and was not in nursing school. She was actually living in America without papers. I found out that all those times she said she was driving, she was actually on a bus. Even though she was undocumented, she was working.

"Whoa. Okay!" I threw up my hands. "That's fine. I will marry you." I shrugged my shoulders. "I mean, I love you. I liked you before you told me all this, so I'm still going to marry you, if that's okay."

But then her mother didn't want her to get married. "He's not the kind of person we want for our daughter," she said.

After that, I moved from that apartment and I went to school in Brookhaven, outside of Dallas. In 2008, I started community college. I didn't have a high school diploma, but because I'd taken five college courses in the military, I no longer needed a high school diploma. I had three As and two Bs.

"Yeah, that's good," the admissions team said.

I earned between 31-35 credits, and then I was eligible to transfer to a four-year university. While I was at Brookhaven, I became the president of international students. That is how I met my next girlfriend, a Korean girl. We dated for two years.

In 2011 I applied to transfer to the University of Texas at Dallas. When I received my acceptance letter, I cried. Every morning I would get up and look at my letter again and say, "So, I'm going to the university." I couldn't believe it. I was finally realizing my vision of going to university. *Thank God. I didn't know I could really do this. But now I'm going.*

When I arrived for orientation, I was so excited to be there. However, as a grown man, looking at these young teenagers, eighteen years old, was kind of shocking. I was in the midst of a group of children.

During that time going to school, I worked as a security officer at McAfee, and that is how I paid my bills.

The University of Texas at Dallas was a tough university, but I made it through. I graduated in December 2013 with a Bachelor's in Political Science.

When I was graduating, I cried because I never thought I could be at the university or earn a degree. Through my tears, I stared at my degree. Seeing the words, "The University of" made me so proud.

Looking at that degree every morning, I started thinking, If I have *this*, I could have my Master's. I didn't know how to do it. Traditional universities were asking for GREs and GMATs, and I didn't have time to write those. Somebody told me I could go to American Military University (AMU), and I found out that AMU didn't have a GRE requirement. I decided I would go there. I went to their website and applied, and after a week or two, I received a letter of acceptance into their master's program to pursue International Relations in Conflict Resolution.

I snapped both my fingers at the same time. "There you go, David," I told myself. "There you go, baby. I got this."

My starting date was January 2014. Just a month after completing my bachelor's, I was starting my master's.

In addition to working on my master's, I also got a job with the Department of Health and Human Services. I started there in 2014 as a Civil Rights Investigator. I investigated complaints people brought to the health care system. We oversaw hospitals, home health agencies, and nursing homes that received financial assistance from the federal government. When these facilities contracted with the federal government, they signed agreements that they would not discriminate against anybody on the basis of race, sex, age, nationality, and sexual orientation. These facilities would agree not to discriminate to receive federal funding, but then they would forget the terms and discriminate against people.

I investigated one case, where someone working for a facility claimed that they refused to treat homosexuals, even though they'd accepted federal money and were bound not to discriminate on the basis of sexual orientation.

The person who was turned away for services, would come to us and file a complaint through our website. I would take that complaint and visit the facility and remind them of their agreement with the government that they would not turn anyone away for services. Then I would ask them what they had to say in their defense. If I found out that they had discriminated against someone, we would charge them or reprimand them. If they did it again, then we shut down the facility.

I had to shut down 15 home health facilities in Houston because those agencies were led by Nigerians who were committing fraud. I didn't want to take away someone's job, but they weren't following the regulations and the laws, so what was I supposed to do?

2015 Trip to Togo and Ghana

In 2015, my mother died, and I went back to Togo for a visit. This was only my second visit back to Togo since I left for the U.S., without saying goodbye to my family. In 2005, while I was still in the military before I got injured, I had a chance to visit.

Now another ten years had passed. I could still hear those Voices from Afar, but they were no longer my age-mates singing the songs they learned at school, but now it was my family, and sometimes strangers, calling to me for help, for money. I thought about my long-ago life as a six-year-old child, working on that mountain while the other kids were in school, and felt a sense of awe that I had succeeded, despite all the obstacles in my way, and that now I am someone they called for help.

The voices calling to me now were the voices of hell and desperation. They wanted financial support. They were not positive voices, but those telling of the pain they were in, how they were struggling to make ends meet.

I traveled back past my old primary school in the town of Warkambou (where my grandfather had lived), and then on to where my father had lived on the outskirts of Warkambou, called Tambisgou. I looked around me in amazement, thinking about how I had been born in this tiny place.

I looked around me, amazed that through all my journey in the U.S., everything here was still the same. The schools where I had grown up were still the same as when I was a kid. They still didn't have libraries. The roads remained unpaved. There was still no electricity.

After my visit to my family, I went on to Ghana. I remembered my first bus trip to Kumasi, the first time I saw a paved road, and I was so awestruck by all the houses and people and cars. Now, going back, after all, I had seen so much more of the world, it doesn't look so beautiful anymore because I have seen many more beautiful things since then.

In Ghana, I saw some friends who still remembered me. "Hey, Yaw," they called me.

I went back to Mr. Appau's house. These people didn't understand children can grow up to become something different. Their only understanding of me was as a laborer, with no parents and no future. Their attitude was "your only future is to weed my farm." I went to his house in Kumasi, to show him how I had changed, but he was in the village.

The person there told me, "They're not here—he and his wife are in the village right now—but I'll tell them you came by."

"Well, okay," I said. I knew the old man must be about ninety years old. But he was still alive, still down at that farm. I knew it would still be a thick forest. And he probably still had some boy there, working for him. That kind of slavery I endured was still going on in Ghana and Ivory Coast where young boys were trafficked to work on cacao farms.

More than anything I wanted to see them face to face. I wanted to see Mr. Appau's wife and tell her who *I* had become and who *she* made me become.

I really wanted to see him. If I would have seen him, I would have given him something.

Even though I hated the way he treated me, I wouldn't have told him off. I had grown up since then, and I remembered what my father said: don't pay back evil with evil. Regardless of what he did, at the end of the day, he prepared me to be who I am today. I've always said that the things you are looking for, those things may not be easy to get. The things you're going through are the foundation to where you want to see yourself. He prepared me for the future.

I believe today that this cruelty was preparing me to be who I am today.

If I had seen him, I would have given him money. He would have been surprised, after all, he did to me.

What they did to me is what made me who I am today. I've always believed that whenever you mistreat somebody, you're not mistreating him. You think you are, but if that person has a vision, if that person is ambitious, he will capitalize on that and become somebody, and then the next time you see him, you will probably bow down. That's my attitude. This is the attitude I carry with me every day, to my work.

I continue to visit Togo every 2 or 3 years and see my family. I also go to Africa often for work. Every year I attend the land force summit with African Land Force commanders.

Preaching in Dallas

While I was working at HHS, I was dating Nicole, a girl from Ghana. I had plenty of money, and our relationship was going well. The job had a two-year term limit, and when that ended, I didn't find another job right away. I found out that the money had meant everything to Nicole. Not having enough money for that girl started to drive me crazy. Just because I didn't have money, so she could have her nails done every week, she suddenly didn't seem to love me anymore. She couldn't get her hair done. I couldn't afford fancy food to put on the table. It became clear to me that we weren't really committed to each other. So, we broke up. I didn't know what to do next. But I swore I wasn't going to date another girl from Ghana, or even West Africa, again.

Even without my job and without Nicole, I was still thinking about school and how I could get to where I wanted to be in life.

I was trying to get a job and surviving on my $700/month check from the VA, so at least I could pay my rent.

The two main jobs I applied for were 1. a quality control inspector for the Department of Commerce and 2. a foreign affairs specialist with the Department of Defense. I received a job offer from the Department of Commerce, but I was still holding out on option 2 because that was more in line with my future track, and it paid more money. The inspector job was rated as GS5, so the money was about $33,000 per year. I would have to go for training, which wasn't in Dallas, where I was living, but they wouldn't pay for my travel. I was dragging my feet on figuring out how to do this training and still hoping the foreign affairs specialist job would come through.

I kept waiting and waiting and waiting to hear from the Department of

Defense, but finally one Friday I decided I was going to have to accept the inspector job. I went to my friend George's apartment and asked him to loan me $500 to fly to the training.

"Hey, George. I got a job. And you know how much my tuition is? They want me to go for training, but I don't have the money."

George clapped his hands together. "No. I will give you five hundred so you can buy a ticket and go there. When everything settles, you can pay me back."

George was a very nice guy, a very good person. I met him at the Sunday soccer park where I played soccer. It was a big group of Ghanaian guys who played soccer and cooked together. They did barbecues. I met this group and became part of them.

Somehow, I got really close to George, maybe because he opened up and started talking to me. We would have conversations. He told me that he shot short comedy videos and invited me to get involved.

"Sure," I said. "Do you need actors? Maybe I can be one of the guys in your show."

"Yes," he said. "I can always use guys who can act."

The most notable video involved me acting as a gay dude. George played opposite me as a Ghanaian who'd come to the U.S. without papers. He wanted to marry someone to become a citizen. He couldn't find a woman to marry him, so he had to marry my character to get a Green Card. In the video, we went through a marriage ceremony together, and when the pastor told him to kiss the bride, he didn't want to kiss me. The immigration officers were standing in the back of the chapel to ensure that the marriage was real, and when he wouldn't kiss me, the gig was up.

We shot that video at George's church, which was called Pentecostal Prayer Ministry. The leader of the church encouraged us to invite more friends to come and help him grow that church into something really big. When we went, there were about twenty people.

"Maybe I can help," I said. "I can support this effort."

Every Sunday I started going to that church. The leader realized I could really speak and had a lot of passion for the Bible. I could explain what the

Bible meant about certain things.

"I want to give you the opportunity to preach next Sunday," he said.

After that, I started preaching every Sunday.

Sometimes we would have revival, and the leader would give me the platform to speak. The people at that church still think I'm a pastor, but I'm not a pastor. I always told them, "I'm not a pastor. I can read the Bible. I can teach you what those words mean. I got the gift, but I'm not a pastor."

One passage I liked to explain was John 3:16. Everyone thinks they understand that passage, but in reality, the message behind it is not just about the love of God. It is more than the love of God. It's way beyond that.

Once I started talking this way, the parishioners would say, "Tell us more."

"God said he sent his only begotten son. Why did he send his son to us? That is like a Christmas gift that someone gives you, right? If somebody gives you a gift, you might have been a very special person. That is why they gave you the gift. When they give you a gift, it is beautifully wrapped. You take the gift, but do you accept that gift first or do you receive it? The box is beautiful. You only receive it, but if you don't see what is inside, how are you going to accept it? So when you open the box, you see, 'oh man, I got an iPhone 12. I love it.' You like it and you start rejoicing, right? Many people have *received* Jesus, but they haven't really *accepted* him because they don't understand what he *carried* with him. What he carried with him is the gift that God gave us, not the person as Jesus. But the message that he carries is what we're supposed to know to understand and fall in love with and be with and eat it and drink it and accept it and make it part of us.

"Huh," those parishioners would say, looking skyward. "We didn't think of it from that perspective."

Since that time, I've been given the gift that God gave me to preach.

George and I were great friends. When I needed a place to crash, I could sleep on his couch. And he was the best cook. There was always plenty of food in his apartment. We'd go there and eat with the other soccer guys. They'd come with the drinks.

No matter what, George was always there for me. He gave me five hundred dollars, and I went to buy a plane ticket. But before I could, I received a phone call. My caller ID labeled it as "unknown," so I didn't pick up. But the caller left a voicemail: "This is your last call, and if we don't hear from you, we are going to move on to another candidate."

What is that? I thought. *Is this some kind of scam?*

I called back the number the person left, though, and asked, "What kind of job is this?"

The man said, "Well, this is the foreign affairs specialist job that you applied for."

I slapped the table. "No way!"

"Yes," the man said. "We've sent you five emails, and you haven't replied, so this was our last time to contact you."

"What? Where did you send those emails?"

"Well, probably check your spam or junk folder."

I found out that the Department of Defense had been emailing me about the internal affairs specialist job and those emails were going to my spam folder, which I wasn't checking. These messages all said that I'd been selected as a foreign affairs specialist to work in San Antonio.

All that time I'd been waiting to hear from them, and those emails had been coming in, one after another, offering me the job. How lucky I was that they called me. They could have just moved on. There are a lot of people waiting in line to get that foreign affairs specialist job. How special I am that they called.

"Hey," they said. "We're going to interview you on Monday." He gave me a time to call, then said, "There's going to be five people in the office that are going to be throwing questions at you. If you do a good job, you'll get it."

Monday I showed up for my interview. Afterward, they said, "You got the job. Congratulations."

My grade started at GS7 and could extend to GS11, after which I could work my way up even higher.

I went back to George's apartment. "Hey, George," I told him. "I got the job."

"Wait," he said. "You went to that training already?"

"No, no. I got the other job. I'm not going to that training after all. I still have the five hundred. The job I'm going to is in San Antonio. So, what am I supposed to do to go to San Antonio?"

George was fully aware that my car had been repossessed because I hadn't been able to keep up on payments.

"It's okay," George said. He loaned me some money to buy a used car. I was able to get a Sonata for four thousand dollars. It was a great car, always running well. I bought it "as is," but it never broke down. This car really helped me.

I said, "God helped me out here. God knows I don't have money. If it breaks down, I wouldn't know how to repair it." But nothing happened to it. I drove it for two years.

"I'm going to drive down to San Antonio," I told George.

In San Antonio, I stayed in a hotel, using the five hundred I had from George to live on while I looked for an apartment. After I got settled with my job, I made a payment arrangement with George and was sending him five hundred a month until I finished paying the money off.

I found an apartment and moved completely to San Antonio. But every weekend I was going back up to Dallas, so I could go to church. I would sleep on George's couch.

During that time, I met Heather, a girl at my church who took videos. I was drawn to her, but she was also so petite, that I thought she was underage. I didn't think I should try to talk to a girl so young. I thought she must be in high school, maybe fourteen years old.

One day in 2017, I was the one preaching, and afterward, I was introduced to her. We were standing in the hallway at the front of the church talking. She was telling me that she was from Namibia in Southern Africa. Namibia is a large country geographically but has a small population of only two million people. The government makes life easy for the people in Namibia so most people from there don't travel much. They have what they need, and they don't want to leave. So right away, I was curious why Heather had left Namibia.

A little girl was interrupting, and Heather told her, "Hey, I'm old. You can't disrespect me."

I looked at the young girl who was probably about eight or nine. I didn't want to ask Heather her age. I was just trying to find it out through investigating her.

"Yes," Heather said. "I'm older than you. I'm old enough I could be your mother."

"Ooooooh," I thought, realizing she was not too young for me. When I realized she was a mature woman, we started talking. I learned that Heather was twenty-seven. After that, we started dating. We agreed that we saw each other as compatible.

Working at the Pentagon

I worked for the Department of Defense as a foreign affairs specialist for two years. I was about to go to General Schedule (GS) 11, a promotion that'd have seen me move up the ladder close to senior leadership. The federal system for job seekers is that if you haven't held any federal job, the system usually puts you at the entry-level from GS-4, GS-5, GS-6, GS-7, GS-9, GS-11 to GS-15 being the highest position a civilian can hold. I saw a job posted on Indeed.com looking for an international affairs specialist at the Pentagon. After I applied, I found out I'd be working as a contractor through a company called Mesmo. I wondered if I should take the risk to leave my federal job and go work as a contractor. I was currently making $50,000 per year, and this job paid about $85,000 per year. The money was good, but what really motivated me to leave my stable federal job for a contracting job was the fact that I was close to actualizing my vision. So, of course, I wanted to grab it. Getting invited to work inside the Pentagon was a dream come true.

I called Mesmo and said, "I'm currently a Foreign Affairs Specialist with the Department of Defense and I'm interested in becoming an International Affairs Specialist."

"You are the kind of guy we're looking for," they told me.

"Really?"

"Yeah." They told me where to go to fill out the application. "Then, when you finish it, let me know," the man said.

Meanwhile, when I was working at my current job, I had to go to a course called Security Cooperation and Planners Course in Carlisle, Pennsylvania taught by Bob Maginnis, a contractor for the Department of Defense.

When I applied for the job with Mesmo, they told me they were going to call Bob Maginnis.

"What?" I said. "Bob Maginnis was my instructor when I went to the Security Cooperation and Planners Course.

"Yes," they said. "He is our (Vice President) VP.

"Really?"

"Yes," they said. "He is going to call you. And he will be the one to interview you."

Bob Maginnis called me the next day at 3:30 PM for the interview.

"Bob Maginnis," I said. "Weren't you my instructor for the Security Cooperation and Planners Course?"

"Yes. Were you there?"

"Yeah."

That was how we began to build our relationship. After that he said, "Send me a writing sample, and after I read that, you'll get a job."

I went back into my office and sent him my writing sample.

He called me again and said, "You got the job. When do you think you can start?"

It was now April 22, 2019.

"We want you here on May 5," he said.

Whoa, I thought. I would have to quickly resign from my federal position and do the paperwork to get out of there. I submitted my letter of resignation and cleared the post.

"Hey guys," I said. "I'm going to start on May 6, 2019. I can't start on the 5th because I have to fly in and get an apartment in Maryland."

I flew out immediately from San Antonio to D.C. to look for an apartment. I got everything ready to move and started my new job on May 6, 2019. Since then, I've been working for Mesmo inside the Pentagon, and here I am today.

All told, even though I suffered through the first years in America, I've now surpassed where I was when I was teaching French in Ghana.

In addition to having my dream job at the Pentagon, I live in a beautiful apartment in Maryland, like the one I saw Mr. Appau living in when I first went to Kumasi.

I attend a charismatic church near my house, but they don't know I can preach yet!

All my life in Africa, voices had been drawing me out of my village, and then out of my country. Now that I'm established in the U.S., these same voices reach back to Africa. There are people I don't know who call me. Some people get my phone number on WhatsApp and call me for money. I don't even know them.

Then, at my job, I work as the African Regional Director, and my portfolio includes all the 54 African countries. My day-to-day operation includes providing analytical support and developing recommendations that inform the execution of and advance U.S. equities in Africa in the form of papers, talking points, read-ahead materials, and participation in meetings.

Moreover, I assist with the development, coordination, and publication of Africa's Strategic Engagement Recommendation that also informs the U.S. Government and Congress about Africa.

I am the planner for the African Land Forces Summit which happens annually on the African continent.

The seventh ALFS was held in Gaborone, Botswana, and co-hosted by the Botswana Defense Force. The 2019 summit was attended by chiefs of land forces from 41 African partner nations, the most ever for ALFS. The theme for the summit was "Strengthening Partner Networks" and the guest of honor was the incoming 37th Vice Chief of Staff of the Army. ALFS participants focused on partner networks and their critical role in providing coordination and collaboration across regional borders for multinational forces.

Furthermore, I provide political-military expertise to the Army Leadership, Staff, and Subordinate Head Quarters on strategic, regional, and country security cooperation issues, I plan, coordinate, and execute Army Staff engagements with senior foreign defense officials and respond to military attaché (MILATT) queries and support foreign embassy functions.

If our generals want to speak to someone on the ground in the African country, I will create the link and make sure that both sides have everything they need to know about each other.

I am an expert in the African region. I help our senior leaders understand the geopolitical landscape along with the cultural aspects of what to say and not to say. I am the man to do all that.

There is a big network of people with whom I communicate. I make a lot of phone calls to Africa and send a lot of emails. I have to talk to the country desk officers, embassies, combatant commanders, army service components, joint staff, state department, and the United States Agency for International Development (USAID).

It would take me about a day to prepare a statement for the Chief of Staff of the army. It goes fast because I send emails letting my network know I need this information by the close of business today. I will get that information as soon as I can.

I have to confirm all the information I receive. All the departments I communicate with have a different focus. When I get their information, I have to make sure that three or four other departments confirm it.

I have to know everything about those fifty-four countries and always wait for a question to come in, and then jump on it, and answer it.

I also handle affairs in the Middle East because the Middle East has some cultural similarities with Africa. I do research and tell the general what he needs to know about that place.

If the Chief of Staff of the Army wants to go someplace, I might have to recommend that he not go to that place. After I list the reasons for not going, he will say, "Okay. Thank you." And he will not go.

Now that I'm living back in Maryland, I'm thinking of going to visit that uncle, the one who "sponsored" me to come to America. He doesn't live far from here. I would like to give him some money. It won't be $10,000, but I would give him something to thank him for bringing me along on my journey.

Every time I get to work, every morning, I'll be smiling, and my boss will be like, "What is wrong with you? You're always smiling. Even when we want you to be upset, you're not getting upset. You're still smiling. You bring positive vibes into the office."

"Sir, that's how I was born."

Being upset with something is not going to change it. It's not going to make you any better of a person. Dwelling on it may make you a worse person. The thing is, it's not going to change anything, so why bother being upset about things? That's how I view the world.

Even now, I'm working at the Pentagon and I'm thinking this is not enough. I want to get somewhere else, but I don't know where I'm going. I feel like I haven't gotten there yet. That is the kind of drive I have.

In 2018, when I moved back to MD, I went on an excursion to Arlington National Cemetery. I wanted to see the fellow fallen soldiers there and pay tribute to them. I was surprised to see that the cemetery was designed exactly how we planted palm trees on Mr. Appau's farm. The way the gravestones were lined up reminded me of the way the palms lined up. I could see a triangle in whichever way I looked. There was beauty and symmetry to this pattern, and I liked how this old pattern met my new life.

Writing My Dissertation

When I was working on my master's at American Military University (AMU), my thesis was titled, "Does the Northern Ireland Peace Process Offer a Model to Resolving Conflict in Africa?" I received an A- on this thesis. I graduated with my Master's in May 2018.

While I was taking my master's, AMU had no doctoral program. Yet, by the time I had completed my master's, they introduced a Doctor of Strategic intelligence and a Doctor of Global Security. I pondered whether or not I should go on to my doctoral degree. I didn't want to wait. The doctoral program would start in September 2018. So, I said, "You know what, I am going to apply. I'm not going to wait. Because if I slow down, I am going to get lazy."

I applied, and they told me they were going to interview me. I went to the interview, and a week later, they said, "Congratulations. You've been accepted into our doctoral program to pursue a doctorate in strategic intelligence."

ATTENDING UNIVERSITY

I slapped my fists on my desk. "Here we go," I said.

I went to AMU in West Virginia on September 2, 2018, to start my first residency. We went through all the drills, heard all their expectations, and expressed our own expectations. We met the faculty and learned the rules. They told us the program was going to be crazy and tough.

"Many of you will drop out," they warned us. "Many of you will go back without completing this program."

Without a doubt, I knew I would not be one of those people to go back. I completed that residency and returned home to my job and work on my doctorate.

After all the crazy things I've been through in my life, I am now in the third year of my doctorate degree and am writing my dissertation. The topic is "Overcoming Security Challenges in West Africa, Through Intelligence Cooperation and Sharing: An exploratory study of Ghana and Nigeria." I am assessing the security challenges in the West African region and how they can better manage the insecurities through intelligence cooperation.

I am busy working through the modifications and revisions suggested by the three people on my dissertation committee. I have a chair, a second reader, and a third reader. The chair and the second reader are from within the school, while the other is from outside the school.

My job is to explain to them what my goal is. If I don't give them a strong goal, they'll toss me around, so I have to be able to argue my point.

When I get done, I expect to have a 300-400-page dissertation.

Ms. Herta Shikongo has been a terrific mentor to me. She tells me when I'm goofing off, and says, "Uh-uh, honey." She points to my desk and says, "Your schoolwork."

She is a computer scientist and works with software. She is very intelligent with computers and helps me with my research software. She helps me obtain graphics and key information.

By the end of 2022, I plan to finish my dissertation and graduate with a doctorate in Strategic Intelligence. The first-ever kind of doctorate in Africa. Being the first in a family of 200 to have gotten up to this level. I'm the only one who has obtained this level of education and been able to come to

America.

Here I am today. But before I close this book, permit me to say this:

I don't believe in dreams, I believe in vision because, unlike dreams, vision provides you with a clear path to arriving at your desired goal. When the time came to action, I didn't hesitate to capitalize on it. I knew very well; that this was the right time to make a move of defying my terrifying father's look to go to school. A renegade or a disobedient child really didn't matter to me because I had an objective to achieve, going to school with my age-mates. I was born into a family that could barely put a $.50 cent food on the table. The two cows I was responsible for could not be sold for food as they were used to plow whenever the rainy season came because, without them, we would have to wait for everyone to finish their work before they could lend us theirs to plow. The season passes by so fast that if one delays when it is raining, they could fall behind and may not get crops or food to feed the family.

Writing this book wasn't easy to put words to paper and detailing every ordeal I've passed through to get to where I am today is refreshing. I hope my story will inspire individuals who find themselves in the same situation to think of executing their own future because no one else will, not even their parents or friends. As a child, I had a vision, and when my father died towards the end of 1993, I quickly realized that I had to get a toolbox and begin to put some tools that may help me execute this vision.

About the Author

David L. Dambre was born in a typical village known as Warkambou, which is located at the extreme border of Ghana and Togo. He grew up in the same village until the age of 17 when he dropped out of 8th Grade. He moved to the United States of America in the early 2000s. Upon arrival, he joined the United States Army and served a tour in Iraq in 2004 and in the Republic of South Korea. David worked at the United States Department of Health and Human Services (HHS) as a Civil Rights Investigator for 2 years from 2014 to 2016 upon the completion of his Bachelor's degree in Political Science from the University of Texas at Dallas. While he was working as a Civil Rights Investigator, he embarked on his graduate studies journey of a Master of Arts in International Relations and Conflict Resolution from the American Military University (AMU). In 2017, he landed another job with the U.S Department of Defense (DOD), Department of the Army as a Foreign Affairs Specialist at the Joint Base San Antonio (JBSA) as Canada Desk Officer in the office of Security Cooperation formally known as G-5. In 2018, he began his doctoral program at the American Military University, specializing in Strategic Intelligence. In 2019, he had an opportunity to work as the African Regional Director at the Pentagon as a contractor with Mesmo, Inc. His portfolio includes all 54 African countries where he works with top African senior military officials. He resigned his federal position to take up the new challenge, the position he has been holding for 3 years now and counting. David is expecting to graduate with a Doctor of Strategic Intelligence (DSI) at the end of 2022.

www.ingramcontent.com/pod-product-compliance
Lightning Source LLC
LaVergne TN
LVHW020443070526
838199LV00063B/4832